Laid Back In
Hollywood

Laid Back In
Hollywood

Remembering

by Patricia Medina Cotten

BELLE PUBLISHING

Printed in the United State of America

Library of Congress Cataloging-in-Publication Data:

Medina, Patricia

    Laid Back in Hollywood: Remembering / by Patricia Medina Cotten.

    p. cm.

    Includes index.

    ISBN 0-964963-51-5

    1. Medina, Patricia 2. Cotten, Joseph 3. Motion picture actors and actresses--United States--Biography. I. Title

    PN2287.M435C68   1998

791.43'028'092   97-77221

ZBI97-2085   CIP

Picture acknowledgements:

From the collections of:

Patricia Medina Cotten's private collection, Marvin Paige, Roger Karnbad, Dorris Halsey and Michael Eldermah.

Belle Publishing
P.O. Box 741010
Los Angeles, CA 90004
(800) 627-0750

Book and cover design by Sparrow Advertising & Design

CONTENTS

Note to Reader

The few dates that I have mentioned are there because they are of the utmost importance to me, and will be so, ad infinitum.

Any remarks about people or places are *not* coincidental, they are intentional.

I have written the truth, so help me God — and, that is the only help I have had.

P.M.C.

Acknowledgements

To the people who stood by me with seeming faith in my eclectic career which came my way with no help or even enthusiasm from me. Can you imagine a "so-called" actress turning down a part opposite John Wayne because she wanted to spend Christmas in England with her family? That really is carrying a mañana attitude a bit far — I didn't regret it. I needed my family and Mr. Wayne did amazingly well without me!

When you are lost and ineffably lonely you think of things that will make your own company bearable. Friends do come. And naturally, friends go. So, in the end, it is you who must live with yourself and if there seems nothing to live for, just remember — remember there once was joy and laughter, so use your nights in drying your pen and maybe your tears will also dry. Maybe . . .

I would like to thank four special friends:

For computer/typing and re-computer/typing and copying my awful handwriting, for becoming part of my days — well, early mornings, anyway, while managing to be a wonderful mother, Linda de Martinez. You know you have my eternal gratitude and I would not like our friendship to end, ever.

Dorris Halsey, I have known you for some years when you handled my Joseph's book so well. We have remained friends and become business partners. You are loyal, clever and extremely brave in accepting me as a client — especially, as you are a literary agent par excellence.

Now, my editor, Margaret Burk. How many nights have we sat together, each with a copy of my rememberings and you have turned to page 151 (or some other page) and gently and securely said, "I would like you to expand this subject"? "But Margaret, I thought editing was *eliminating*." "Just think about it and if you agree, do as I say. You see, dear, editing has many meanings." It does? How we laughed and worked into the night. And how charming and gracious you were while always getting your way. I am going to miss those evenings. When we first met, I never for a second thought that we would become practically related. Thank you for your patience, for cheering me up when I got depressed and for just being you. A gracious lady who knew how to handle a spoiled, difficult, depressed and lazy woman.

Dear Ruthie Esmond: What would I do without your daily criticism and encouragement? You made me laugh when I wanted to cry. Your talent for listening as I read paragraph after paragraph over the telephone was such an encouragement to me. Thank you for being that friend in my time of need — don't think it won't happen again!

Thank you, all four of you, from the bottom of my damaged heart.

P.M.C.

Prologue

I suppose I am alive in this aloneness. It embraces my whole being like a frozen fire. I am ablaze, but it's cold. My heart is beating so loudly that I feel as if I'm running in a marathon.

Why am I running forward? There's nothing there; only more aloneness. Have I always been alone? What is happening to me? I must have lost someone.

Now I'm running backwards, seeming to know where I'm going.

Months, yes months, like pages turning, appear to be the awakening of my mind. I have lost my whole world, but I am beginning to see the pages and it is all unravelling before my eyes.

My arms ache, for they have clung so long. My lips are speechless for they have tasted so much passion.

Passion?

Yes, I have lost someone.

The months stop. It is 1994 — such a hazy date. But the heavens open with an enormous flash of lightning.

Instantly, my arms stop aching and I reach for the light. It is warm, almost an earthly warmth. And I behold a vision appearing.

It is a vision.

Through this unreal light, I hear his voice, "Patricia. Hello, little thing."

"Who is it?" I whisper, fearing I'm dreaming.

"This is your husband. Joseph Cotten."

I see his face. That face that has crowded my dreams and haunted my loneliness.

"Oh, Jo, why did you leave me? I can't go on without you."

"Only my physical being had to leave you."

I start to cry. Soon I'm crying like a child. I am a child, sobbing uncontrollably.

I almost feel him touch me.

"I'll always watch over you. But, Patricia, you had a life before me. Remember it all. Then remember our years together and how powerful our love was. Wrap yourself in my love and know that I'm giving you strength to be happy. Though my being has disappeared, my love endures."

And as he disappears, the lightning also disappears. The light becomes real and natural. My tears have stopped. I am a young girl in an earlier time. You see, I haven't met him yet.

Book One

The Living Was Easy

- 1 -

Yesterday

I was born in England a long time ago. My mother was English. Thoroughly English. In fact, so thoroughly English it is incredible that she married a Spaniard.

They were the most mis-matched couple it has ever been my pleasure to know. But they had a good marriage, and in their independently foreign way, they loved each other.

When they met he couldn't speak English and she couldn't speak Spanish. They handled their courtship in French.

At a suitable time after the nuptials, my mother gave birth to the first of their three sensational daughters. They named her Pepita (for my father's mother), but as soon as she was able, she gave herself the name Piti.

Since she christened herself very wisely, that became the name we all call her. Piti she was, and Piti she is.

Not long after Piti made her presence felt, I burst upon the scene, and since I was such an adorable child, it took no time for me to choose my own name. Probably in competition with Piti's tiny name, I demanded to be called 'Patricia.' Nobody debated it. However, when some years later a third daughter arrived upon the threshold, Mummy named her 'Gloria' in such a way that everyone including Gloria knew that there would be trouble if she chose to be known by any other name.

I don't know how much influence my mother's putting an end to this name calling of her girls had on her or their decision, or even if it was a decision, but they did not have any more children, which was fine by us. We were enough.

My sisters and I have always been the very best friends. There has never been a time that I have considered anyone in the world a better friend than either Piti or Gloria.

We had a happy childhood, showered with love in a beautiful house. We were not poor in any sense of the word. We spoke Spanish and English. Piti and I learned French at school, and then much later on, I learned Italian.

Our home was in Stanmore about an hour from London, and it was extremely large. In the entrance hall we had a huge, very realistic, stuffed bear. He was quite beautiful. All the rooms were big, which was just as well, because being a musical family, we had six grand pianos in the house (all in different rooms, of course) and a spinet. *Now* I wonder why we never questioned having so many. Piti would be playing beautifully in one room, Glory would be playing quite poorly but singing marvelously in another. She had inherited her coloratura voice from Daddy whose beautiful tenor voice had often filled La Scala in Milan. He sang under the name 'Nevotti.' No one asked him why he didn't use his own name, but it might have been because Italian tenors were more popular than Spanish ones. This was long before Placido Domingo.

Aside from all the happy noises going on in the house, we did have a flourishing garden, and, quite far from the house, the most unusually pretty stables. Although Mummy and Daddy disagreed on the imminence of war in the late 30's, they did agree that we shouldn't keep horses, so it was remodeled into a house for the few people that were left working for us. This didn't last long because when war was declared, we had to move to our flat in London, and "Herondale" (named for herons: beautiful, fluffy, feathered birds) was requisitioned by the R.A.F.

Before the war, we used to rent a house in North Wales for three months in the summer. The three of us would ride horses along the beach. Gloria being 'the baby' still (well, 'child' anyway) got to ride a pony. She was the best rider of the three of us. We had a riding instructor whom we called Punch. I don't think any of us knew his real name. He had a large nose and bow legs and was not quite as tall as I.

As I have said, Gloria was the best rider. Piti rode in a rather dignified way and always with a long rein. Apparently, no one had told me I wasn't a jockey, so I would ride very far forward on the horse's neck and gallop wildly and dangerously along the sand. Both of my legs were on either side of the horse, so I had the horse's neck in between my legs. That area is called "the fork." Punch would catch up with me yelling, "Easy on your fork, Miss Patricia!" He said this so often that the others would tease me and imitate him.

What I didn't realize, but Piti and Gloria did, *was* that Punch had a violent crush on me. One day, when we got back from our ride, I was picking peas that were going to be cooked for dinner. Out of the blue sprang Punch. He grabbed hold of me and kissed me in the cabbage patch. (He *kissed* me on the mouth but I was in the cabbage patch.) Without knowing what I was doing, I lifted my knee and aimed directly at his groin! He fell right there in our kitchen garden, and I left him moaning in agony as I ran into the house in floods of frightened tears.

Mummy found me shaking with fear. She made me tell her what happened. That was the last of poor Punch! But I really was very young.

"I hope you slapped him very hard," said Mummy.

"No, I lifted my knee and hit him hard *there*. I left him screaming."

Mummy went ashen. "Go to your room. I'll talk to you later," said my wise mother.

Our father was an intellectual. History, poetry and, of course, music were his life.

Although small talk bored him, he had a wicked sense of humor. Daddy was fortunate in not having to work. He was a barrister but he never practiced. He sang gloriously when he was invited to do so.

My mother was tall, beautiful and very musical. She had the best sense of humor of all of us. No one could touch the wit and grace with which she could turn a phrase.

Mummy told us all that age was the most private thing a woman can have. "Only divulge it to your physician. All of you forget your ages. You will find, as you grow older, no one with manners will ask you how old you are." We have obeyed her without any difficulty or criticism!

We all had a big surprise. Actually, it was a shock when we took our annual holiday to Paris and loaned our country house to a film producer and his family. His name was Joe Rock and he owned a studio in Elstree. I still had a few more years to spend at school, however, when he saw me running around the house, he looked at me and told my parents something like, "That girl would look great in pictures."

I probably wasn't running around the house, I was more likely tossing my hair and smiling too often, being aware that he was someone rare I had never met nor heard of. *A Film Producer!*

His remark about my looking great in pictures did not indeed delight Mummy and Daddy. They did, however, succumb to his charm and agreed that *when* I left school he could make a test of me. My sisters found this all exceedingly humorous and teased me all the time by calling me "Film star, film star!"

The teasing soon ceased when Piti and I returned to Tolmers Park, our boarding school. Since it was the best school in England, and Mummy was rather a snob, that's where she sent us.

* * *

Tolmers Park was a beautiful estate in Hertfordshire, reputed to have been given to the Earl of Essex by Queen Elizabeth I. Essex is known worldwide as being one of her favorite courtiers. She made handsome gifts such as this fabulous building and land to several people during her long reign.

The head mistress, Miss Whittle, adored Piti who was good at everything she undertook, particularly poetry and English literature. She also was still very musical and played the piano with great ease.

I was only interested in art. I had an ally in the mistress who was in charge of drawing and painting, however, Miss Whittle cared for me not at all. She would accuse me of wearing "make-up" (which I didn't have, so, obviously, didn't use). But several times when it was my misfortune to run into Ethel Whittle in the passages, she would pull a handful of Kleenex out of her handbag which she carried constantly (not unlike the Queen) and rub my eyebrows and lips very hard. I only tolerated this because of the expression on her face when she found the Kleenex remained white. My eyebrows remained black and my lips which had become redder after the treatment gave a triumphant, malevolent smile.

Poor Miss Whittle. She was really very nice and I was quite glad that Piti's charm made up for my clumsiness and lack of interest in any lessons.

We shared a room, the two of us. Spoiled sisters, happy in each other's company.

One night when we were in our pajamas and waiting for matron to order us to bed, Piti was writing on a piece of paper. When she finished it she read it to herself then got up and started to leave the room.

"Where are you going?" I said.

"Miss Black asked me to take this poem to her in her study when I finished it. She thinks I'm quite a poet."

Off she trotted to the English teacher, holding her latest poem carefully. A short while later she came dashing back into the bedroom, and flung herself on her bed in floods of tears.

"What happened, Piti? Oh, what happened?" I cried. I was dreadfully upset, for Piti was, and always had been, a very brave person.

I put my arms around her and she sobbed on my shoulder. At that point, matron walked into the room. She grabbed hold of Piti, pushed her hair back and tried to stem the interminable flood of tears that poured down her little face.

"What happened?" asked matron.

No reply. Just more tears, and she shook her head.

"Please, dear. Tell me what happened?"

Matron finally turned to me and repeated the question.

"Well, matron, she was taking her new poem down to show Miss Black and — I don't know what could have happened." I was beginning to cry.

Piti got up and walked over to the wash bowl. She washed her mouth over and over again.

"When you showed your poem to Miss Black, what happened? You did show it to her?"

Piti nodded her head, then flung herself on the bed. Matron drew up a chair and sat down.

"I'm not going to leave this room until you tell me exactly why you are so upset."

After a while Piti looked at matron and whispered, "She kissed me."

"Did she read the poem and then kiss you on the cheek?"

"She didn't read the poem. She took me in her arms and she kissed me in a disgusting way." She started spitting on the floor and crying again.

I noisily joined in the crying until matron told me quite severely to keep quiet.

"Get into bed, Piti. This will never happen again. Try and settle down. Your sister is with you. Thank you for telling me about it." She covered her up, patted her head, walked quietly out of the room and closed the door.

We didn't discuss it. Poor little innocents — we just lay awake wondering.

The following morning, Piti was summoned into Miss Whittle's study. Matron was there. Miss Whittle told Piti that she had just been kissed because she was clever and it was an affectionate appreciation for her talent. Piti said nothing. Matron said it all. (We used to call Matron "Jam Pot" because she was short and fat.) I should like to belatedly say to her here and now:

"Dear Jam Pot, you were a good woman, a brave, sweet normal woman. You loved your pupils and you had the guts to protect them. Thank you."

I hope my words reach her.

Next term, there was no sign of Miss Black. Another English mistress had taken her place.

* * *

At Tolmers in the hunting season, we would have "Meets" every weekend. "Meets" has many meanings. The one aptly described in *Webster's International Dictionary,* "A meeting of horses and hounds for hunting," clarifies it for people who are confused by the expression. Our "Meets" at this splendid estate were a sight to behold — the men in their red coats, gathered on their horses in the driveway. Quite a few of our Tolmers' pupils joined the group.

Piti didn't always ride, but she was needed there as she had now become "head girl." She'd been a prefect long enough to qualify. She was very pretty, smaller and slimmer than I, and much more charming.

"Meet" weekends, I would sneak into the fields far down on our huge school property and paint.

One Saturday, I was painting happily in the private haven that I had discovered. I leaned back to look at my canvas.

Suddenly, I heard a voice say: "Now, that is quite beautiful."

I looked around and saw an extremely handsome young man smiling at me.

"You're an artist," he said.

Since that didn't sound like a question, I didn't disagree.

"I haven't finished," I said, trying to hide my moderately good painting.

"Perhaps you need a rest," he said, and then, "how about a cigarette?"

"Thank you," I heard myself say as I took a cigarette out of his case and tried very hard to stop my hand from shaking while he lit it.

I felt very sophisticated and took in a huge puff using every vestige of willpower that I owned. I did not throw up — but I almost died. I could hear my sisters laughing at me and calling me a "show off."

I was about to get up and lean on a nearby tree when he asked, "Do you come here often?"

I took another painful puff on my cigarette and said, "Whenever I can steal away."

"Do you want to put your cigarette out?"

"Yes, please."

"How old are you?"

"Mummy told us never to tell our age."

"That would be when your about twenty. How old are you now? Sixteen?"

I hesitated, but knowing I must have gone very pale, "I'm fourteen-and-a-half."

He smiled, such a nice smile, and said, "You look older and you're very beautiful."

"I shouldn't be here, and I shouldn't be talking to you. I could get into trouble."

I had a bright red smock over my uniform, so I could be any age and come from anywhere.

"Would it upset you to get into trouble?"

"Not really. I seem always to be doing the wrong thing."

"Are you at school at Tolmers Park?"

"Yes."

"Shouldn't you be at the 'Meet'?"

"Yes."

We both looked at each other and laughed.

"My name is John and I'm twenty-two."

"I'm Patricia and you already know my age."

I decided not to paint anymore.

"Are you going away now?" asked John.

"Yes, I'd better get back before anyone discovers my hiding place."

"I saw two girls walking behind those bushes, you'd better wait a bit," he said.

"Oh dear, school is such a bore." I started to collect my paints and brushes. John folded my easel and started to walk beside me.

"Don't come with me, please. We'll get arrested."

"Arrested!" he almost shouted and laughed quite loudly. Then he handed me my easel.

I looked back at him. He was smiling at me: "I wish I were older," I said.

"Why? Fourteen is a fine age."

"Yes, but if I were older I could smoke properly and you could marry me."

Dropping my paints as I ran in embarrassment, I distinctly heard him call out, "I'll wait for you, little artist."

* * *

There was a movie that night for prefects and, of course, Piti, the head girl. When Piti came to bed I was already asleep. I didn't get to tell her about my adventure, *but* . . .

The next morning, as usual, we all attended prayers. And, as usual, after prayers, Miss Whittle made a very short little speech. The speech she made that morning went thus!

"It came to the attention of our head girl that someone from this school was seen smoking on the grounds yesterday. Naturally, she reported it to me. Now I leave it up to the honesty of the culprit to come to me and own up. Breaking of the rules cannot go unpunished."

To say I was stunned is putting it mildly. It was a long time before I could get Piti on her own. When I did, it certainly "hit the fan!"

"How could it be you? Where on earth did you get a cigarette?"

"A very nice young man gave it to me."

"Oh! No! Where did you find a young man, nice or not?" she snapped.

"I'm not going to tell you. Fancy reporting your sister!"

"I didn't know it was you."

"Well, anyway, I hate you. Why shouldn't I try a cigarette?"

"Because you're too young and you're at school."

"I'll have to go and own up to old Ethel Whittle and tell her my own darling sister reported me."

"I did not report you, Pat. I had no idea it was you. Now pull yourself together and let's make a plan."

"Maybe you could get me expelled. I'd love that."

"Don't be ridiculous. I have an idea. You'll have to go and own up. What was that play we saw in the holidays? 'As You Like It,' wasn't it?"

"You liked it better than I did!"

"Never mind, come on. Let's go to Ethel now. I'll come with you."

Piti knocked on the door and the two sisters, temporarily hating each other, walked into the inner sanctum.

Ethel Whittle looked rather startled to see the two of us — and looking so serious.

"Miss Whittle, I was the girl who was smoking yesterday," I said as contritely as I could.

"Well, how wrong of you, and how difficult for your poor sister to have to report you."

Piti tried to interrupt but Ethel had just got going. She looked at me with disdain and said, "I'm going to ask your sister to suggest a punishment, so that you will never make that mistake again."

Piti's voice was loud and clear and quite stern. "Miss Whittle, we are planning to go and see *As You Like It* during our three weeks holiday. I don't like to suggest it, but I think Pat — eh — Patricia would be very upset if she weren't allowed to attend."

"That is your punishment," said Ethel to me as I burst into floods of overdone tears. "You cannot go and see *As You Like It*."

I continued my howling as we were dismissed and Piti led me from the room.

"You didn't have to make such a noise."

"I wanted to appear truly heartbroken."

Piti put her arm round me, she giggled and said, "Maybe I should go back and own up that you've already seen *As You Like It*."

I smiled and put my arm round her. "I hated the cigarette," I said.

"What about the young man?" said Piti.

"He's my secret — you find your own young man." I started to twirl her round —

"Oh, I will. I most certainly will as soon as I leave here."

We continued to twirl.

"Oh, Piti, don't leave before I do."

"I'm afraid I'll have to, but I'll do my best to get you out. I'll work on Mummy and Daddy."

"I couldn't stand it without you, even though you're a beast."

"I'm not. I'm your best friend."

"That you are." One more twirl.

* * *

Piti did leave school quite abruptly the following term. Rather than have an unfortunate discussion with our parents, she took matters into her own hands. She waited until we landed in Miss Whittle's study and made her announcement. There and then she collected her bags and no one argued with her except me.

She walked out to the car with her suitcases. She shook hands with Miss Whittle, put her arms around me as she saw the real tears appearing.

"I have to do this, darling, or I'll be here forever. Try and be good. You are very clever and I'll never stop trying to get you out."

I ran after the car as it drove away. Mummy and Daddy waving, and I saw Piti put her hands over her face and I knew she was crying too.

After she left I was so miserable and such a nuisance for several months that finally both the school and my parents agreed that I should leave.

I did not forget John. In fact, when Piti left school, we met in my haven a few more times. No more cigarettes. He did kiss me once. I almost fainted and fell. After he got me back on my feet, I never went there again. I was tragically, ineffably embarrassed.

"The Odd Couple" — my beloved mother and father.

- 2 -

Love and War and Marriage

Once home and out of uniform, with a little lipstick and her long, thick black hair flowing, Piti found plenty of young men. She kept them at arm's length until — Ken and Desmond. She had to decide between the two, and she did. She made the right choice. I wanted to hear more about it, but that day my parents had promised I would go to Rock Studios and make my screen test.

I remember I wore a revealing wine-colored dress. I had had an argument with my mother since leaving school because she wouldn't let me wear a bra. Even at thirteen and fourteen when I met John, the first love of my life, he thought I looked older. Perhaps beneath my smock a small mountain of breasts had given him that impression.

* * *

Going to the studio was very scary for me, and I made, I think, the worst screen test that was ever made. My mind was on many other things, and I was tearful. I wanted to hear Piti's decision about whom she would marry . . . I wanted to be with Gloria, who was now pretty and interesting and funny. My future was the farthest thought from my mind.

Although Desmond was very attractive, there was something much more interesting and exciting about Ken. He was, and is, a marvelous pianist. There was no doubt left in her mind. Ken proposed and she accepted.

Ken had joined up in the 11th Hussars, one of the most famous regiments in England. They also were referred to as the "Cherry Pickers," because, when not at the front, they changed into cherry-colored trousers in the evening. As the war was now going great guns, Ken would be called away any time, therefore, they had a short engagement and a long and beautiful wedding.

He was stationed all round England for about a year, constantly awaiting his call.

The Air Force had requisitioned our large house in Stanmore, so Mummy, Gloria and I lived in a flat in Hamilton Terrace, London. Daddy had gone to visit his family in Spain and, suddenly, the war started. Being Spanish, and Spain being pro-German, Daddy was kept as a political prisoner for the entire duration of the war. Mummy was without her husband for all those years.

* * *

At about 1:00 A.M. one morning, Piti called from some God forsaken place in England and said she was in labor.

"What shall I do, Pat? I've tried to call Ken and he's on duty. I have to get to London to the nursing home."

"Call Ken again, and tell them it's an emergency. You'll get him. Then drive slowly to London and I'll get in touch with the nursing home. They'll have your room ready and the doctor and nurses will be awaiting your arrival . . . and your baby's," said the voice of authority, her younger sister!

She did exactly as I told her to do. She and Ken arrived in London in enough time for Piti and me to go and buy a pair of slippers, which she apparently needed. Then we went straight to the nursing home where tiny little Piti gave birth to a seven pound baby girl. It was a natural birth. Her name is Jennifer. (She is now a very attractive young woman with children of her own.)

Ken told me he had just been called to the front and was worried about telling Piti. Finally, of course, he had to tell her. When he left, Piti and Jenny moved back to our family.

"I'm going to join him Pat," Piti would constantly say. I would agree. What else could I do?

Finally, she managed to get a berth on a ship by evacuating her baby from England and the bombs.

The ship was to leave from Liverpool. Mummy and I went up with her. We were not allowed on the ship, so we said our good byes to her at the Adelphi Hotel where we were spending the night.

I do not remember the date, but it was the worst bombing of Liverpool docks in the entire war.

A loud voice ordered us down to the cellar immediately. The noise of crashing buildings and glass and ships was horrendous. Mummy was sobbing incessantly, saying, "Oh, my poor little Piti. Dear God, we've lost her."

Naturally, I spent the night crying too. The bombs were incessant. I couldn't imagine any of the ships escaping those deadly weapons. I wasn't too sure about the hotel, either.

Daylight: The raid was over. Rain and a terrible quiet. From nowhere appeared a very young dirty little boy.

"Mrs. Medina," he called.

Frightened, Mummy whispered, "I am she."

He gave her a little piece of paper. On it was scrawled, "I'm alright. Piti."

We thanked God. We wondered where she found the youngster and the bit of paper. Did it matter? She had survived the worst bombing of the docks. It was obvious that that fiend Hitler had his German forces escalating. In fact, the war was escalating rapidly. I prayed that there would always be an England.

* * *

Back to London and more bombs —

Mummy was very happy to have an invitation from the Younghams, friends of hers who lived in the country. They invited us to go one Sunday for lunch and tea. We would have to go by train because of the petrol rationing. Mr. Youngham would meet us at the station upon arrival, and when we left he would take us to the station so that we could get home before blackout.

* * *

It was a fresh sunny day and Mummy looked very pretty dressed up for a change. I was now wearing lipstick, and I wore a lovely red woolen dress that Piti had bought me before she took off in search of Ken.

There were no taxis. We had to take a bus to the station. We just caught the train and settled down in the dingy compartment that was to take us to the country air.

Mr. Youngham was delightful. He was so sweet to Mummy who must have been more lonely than she showed. Daddy, a prisoner in Spain; Piti and Ken, God knows where. Ken fighting for his country and Piti and her baby on their way to South Africa in search of news of him.

Mummy only had me to lean on and at that time I didn't realize how lost she must have felt. She feared the bombs dreadfully and was so relieved to be in the quiet of the country.

It was a short trip to their home, which was a large old Tudor house surrounded by what seemed like an old-fashioned country garden. Mrs. Youngham was very attractive: tall, blondish and slim. She and Mummy were both wonderful looking and they seemed so happy to be together.

I'm sure Mummy was glad to feel compassion from an old friend who was luckier than she, as her husband was at her side. Watching them, I became aware that it wasn't my company that Mummy needed. She was still young and lovely and she desperately needed her husband. I prayed that he'd come back soon.

"It's been such ages since we've seen each other," said Mrs. Youngham. "What a pretty daughter you have. Is this Patricia?" she said.

As I replied to her, the French windows opened from the garden and in walked *John*. I remembered my behavior when he kissed me and I was afraid he did too. I was just shaking hands with his mother. She must have thought me a most affectionate or nervous girl, for I clung to her hand tightly as I absorbed the shock.

"Darling, you haven't met Mrs. Medina and her daughter, Patricia," she said to him.

With absolutely no sign of recognition, he first greeted Mummy and then came over to me.

"How do you do. What did Mother say your name was?"

"Patricia," I replied in a voice that seemed not to belong to me.

Mr. Youngham brought a magnum of champagne, poured a glass for all the grown-ups and one for John.

"Help John pass them around, dear," said my mother.

I walked over to the sideboard.

"Give Patricia some juice," said his mother.

At the sideboard, he stood behind me to hide me from the others and gave me a small glass of champagne which I swallowed in a gulp. I took Mummy her champagne and shakily carried my dreary glass of juice — but the champagne he'd sneaked for me warmed my stomach and gave me a little courage.

They had chickens and a vegetable garden, so we had a lovely lunch: roast chicken, roast potatoes and peas. Such a special treat in war-torn, rationed England

After lunch, they offered to give me a few eggs to take home. Mummy's eyes were shining. How long since she'd eaten an egg? We had no chickens as we didn't live in the country. Eggs had become a memory.

John announced that he'd go out and see if there were any eggs.

"Patricia, would you like to come and help me? I'm clumsy with eggs." He held the French doors open for me as I stepped out into the garden without looking at him.

Once outside, he took my hand. "Come, let's get away from the house. We can pretend to look at the chickens. They're very boring."

"What are you doing here?" said I, stupidly.

"I live here. It's not too far from where you were at school."

"Of course."

He put an arm round my shoulders. "You're growing up. I can't kiss you with that lipstick on."

"I shouldn't think you'd want to kiss me again."

"You shouldn't think," he replied. He took a handkerchief out of his pocket, blotted my lips and kissed me gently.

He dropped a piece of paper out of his pocket. I picked it up. He grabbed it from me.

"What is it?"

"Nothing."

"You're hiding something from me."

"There's a war on. I'm an Englishman."

"Oh, no," I cried. "You're not going to fight?"

"I have to."

I started to cry. He just looked at me and said nothing.

"You think I'm very silly, don't you?" still crying.

He cradled my face in his hands and said, "One day I'll tell you what I really think of you, little artist."

We heard voices from the house.

"Quick, get the eggs," I said.

He didn't move. He looked so sad, but he still held my face. "Did you hear what I said?"

"Yes. You'd tell me what you really think of me. Tell me now."

"When I come back."

He wiped my eyes and we got the eggs in silence.

Back at the house, we had tea. Then, Mr. Youngham got the car.

"Would you like me to come with you, Dad?" said John.

"Yes," he answered.

It was a short drive. John and I sat in the back seat. He held my hand.

The train was already at the station. Mummy was being rushed to the train by Mr. Youngham.

John turned my hand over, kissed the inside, then closed it. "Take that with you," he whispered as he pushed me on the train behind Mummy.

They waved us off. I kept my hand tightly closed. I didn't want that kiss to escape. It was my most precious possession. If I had to open my hand, I would first stroke my face, so that I would feel his gentle kiss. That night I would not wash my face.

"You'll be back just in time to hear Churchill," John's father yelled.

All of England was dependent on Winston Churchill, our beloved Prime Minister. He was eloquent beyond imagination and an anchor for every Britisher. We all were targets for the German planes. They were far stronger than we, stronger in the air and in manpower, but in "belief," we had the edge. Mummy would turn on the six o'clock news every night, and Churchill would speak at the end of the broadcast. Gloria and I would sit on the floor and listen. And if we didn't understand that dreadful war, we understood the words "We will *never give in.*"

On the train, Mummy, in her wisdom, said, "That young man was very sweet to you. Have you met him before?"

"Yes."

"Where? They live not far from Tolmers Park?"

"I met him there at a Meet."

"He's joined the Navy. Did you know?"

I turned my face to the window, but I think she saw the reflection of my tears.

She put her arms round me, "Darling little Patsy, they're all going, all the flowers of our youth. We must pray for John and all the others as well."

I now cried openly in her arms.

What a wonderful woman was my mother. There was no one for her to lean on, yet she felt my youthful sorrow.

* * *

The Germans bombed day and night — our poor little R.A.F. that Churchill so aptly named "The First of the Few." I called them "little" which seems like a misnomer, but, you see, they were so very few, and so gloriously, sometimes tragically, brave. "Little" seemed to embrace the whole force.

Many people would take blankets and spend the night in the underground. Down there they felt, and most were, safe from the bombs. Mummy, Gloria and I stayed in our completely blacked-out flat; Gloria had just come back from school because it closed due to the air-raids.

It was a terrible time for everyone in England.

We couldn't get food except with our ration books. A tiny piece of meat for a family for a week — no eggs — milk, only for babies.

Gloria and I became very, very hungry. One night, lying in our beds, we were whispering to each other, as Mummy was asleep in the other room. Gloria kept saying, "Oh, Pat. I'm so hungry."

I replied, "So am I."

We got up, crept into the kitchen, and found the little piece of meat which was our ration for the week. Mummy had cooked it. We got two slabs each of black bread, which was the only bread we could get. We made ourselves a couple of sandwiches and we had a real midnight feast. It was wonderful.

We crept back to bed, nourished and happy and both fell asleep.

In the morning, we were awakened by the sound of Mummy weeping. She couldn't find any food to give us.

Feeling rightfully guilty, I got up, ran all the way to the butcher's and got in line in the queue.

When I reached the butcher, he said, "Where are your ration books?"

I was almost in tears and said, "I'm afraid we've eaten our ration for this week. It's a very sad story, sir."

"What do you expect me to do about it?" he said, gruffly.

"I don't know, but my sister and I stole it and Mummy's crying."

"Come in the back door," he whispered. He attended to the rest of the people, then he looked at me standing in his shop.

He got a huge knife, cut off a nice large chunk of meat, wrapped it in a piece of newspaper, placed it in my trembling hands and said, "There you are, my little luv. Take that 'ome to your Mum."

Well, I ran home faster than I had run to the butcher's.

When I gave it to Mummy, she just stared unbelievably at it. She couldn't understand where it had come from. She asked me how I got it, and I told her.

The crying was over. We said she could have it all, which, of course, she didn't. She made us a lovely meal — this time, to last us the week!

The butcher became a hero. We blessed him with every mouthful.

* * *

When the post arrived that day there was a parcel for me. It was a small gold cigarette case. There was a note inside. It said, "For my beautiful little artist. I noticed you have not taken to smoking so you can use this as a compact to check that no one touches your lipstick! I am now in the Navy. We are not out at sea with most of the Home Fleet but in the harbour and at anchor at Scapa Flow. So please write to me here c/o The Royal Oak. She is a fine ship. Love, John. P.S. Are you of marriagable age yet? I'm still waiting."

I wrote him a letter immediately and told him to hurry home as I was getting old waiting for him to marry me.

I rushed out and posted the letter.

When I returned, Mummy was listening to the wireless. We never called it the "radio."

"This is the six o'clock news. While most of the Home Fleet was at sea, a German submarine breached the defenses at Scapa Flow where the Royal Oak was in harbor at anchor. She was torpedoed three times, lost and sank immediately. The Prime Minister will speak at the end of the news. . ."

I turned off the wireless and ran to Mummy.

Gloria said, "Was John on the Royal Oak? Were you going to marry him?"

Poor little Gloria adored me and thought I was really going to get married to John — so did I!

Mummy, as always, came to the rescue. "Darling, he was the first boy you met, and he was wonderful." She poured me a neat scotch (we had half a bottle for months). "Drink that, darling. There, have a good cry while I write to his mother. He didn't suffer, my pet. There'll be other boys you'll like and lose. We must be as brave as John was."

I cried myself to sleep. Of course, I'd never care for anyone else. My young heart was broken.

Tomorrow was another day and we were in danger all the time. I saw Mummy's sad face and went and put my arms around her. Gloria joined us and we all hugged each other while the country was tottering, fighting alone.

I turned on Churchill and we listened to his voice. The voice that carried us through the heartbreak and the devastation.

* * *

One night, quite early, we heard the very distinctive sound the Luftwaffer's engines made, quite different from our own precious planes.

We sat close together in the lonely, completely blacked-out living room. We even turned off the one light we were allowed. Suddenly, Gloria marched up to the windows, opened the black out and the windows themselves, and sang "Ave Maria" at the top of her beautiful coloratura voice.

The *moment* she finished, the "All Clear" rang out. It is a moment I shall never forget. I felt so proud of my young sister. She attacked the enemy in her own wondrous way.

Because of our defense, and the miraculous accuracy and tenacity of all our forces, they had to give us a rest from time to time. While thinking up some new and terrifying form of bombing during these seemingly quiet spells, we tried to live a normal life.

* * *

In spite of my dreadful test at the Rock Studios, they did offer me a contract, which my mother and father refused. That was presumably going to be the end of my career as an actress. Even if I'd been interested and had shown some talent in my test, I would not have argued with my parents about such an important step in my life.

Having given up painting several times, I decided I wanted to be a doctor. But still there was the film offer, and it became rather interesting, this idea of being an actress. I began to see myself in the mirror in a different way.

And as we had lived near Elstree, where most of the studios were in England, and I was contacted by an agent who had seen my horrendous effort. I was offered a small part as a Spanish girl. The part was so small that the moment I came on the screen, I was shot. I cannot remember the film. They probably wisely cut me out. I was offered and accepted two or three other parts — real parts — and I found myself improving.

* * *

The director of the last picture gave a little dinner party. I sat next to a young and exceedingly handsome actor who, being an Englishman, had returned from Hollywood to join up and do his bit in WWII.

His name was Richard Greene, and he had starred in quite a few big films, especially for his age. I admired him for giving it up and being patriotic. I hoped we'd have an interesting meeting and become friends, but when he started making conversation, we disagreed with each other intensely. About three weeks later, we got married.

Every night during the bombing I had been out flirting with all the attractive men "on leave" in England. I didn't know a thing about getting married, but I was, at that time

My first husband, Richard Greene. We were too young for marriage, but there was nothing wrong with my eyesight!

(without any modesty), a very pretty girl, and I had had about five proposals (of marriage!). I very much enjoyed the admiration and even gave the impression that I would consider marriage with several of them. I probably was the most talked about girl in London — all talk and no action. Mummy had to let me go out as they were nice young men. We wouldn't go out during an air-raid, but, of course, while we were dancing, it seems the raids would start. We refused to be intimidated and some of us were lucky. I would telephone Mummy to say I was all right.

Richard proposed to me one afternoon when we were having tea at the Berkley Hotel. Together we went to the telephone and I said, "Mummy, I'm engaged."

"What, again?" was her honest and unfortunate response.

* * *

We wed in St. James, Spanish Place, the most famous Catholic church in England. Richard was a Catholic, which had surprised me. I knew he was Irish, but we hadn't discussed religion; we really didn't know each other very well!

Mummy and I spent the night before the wedding at the Mayfair Hotel. We were having the reception there after the wedding, so it seemed sensible to move in until after we were married.

Of course, I didn't sleep a wink. I asked Mummy one million questions pertaining to 'first night' sex — was I to contribute? My limited experience was what was so unattractively referred to as 'necking'.

Mummy helped me not at all. "It's all natural. You'll find out. Now go to sleep. You won't look beautiful if you don't sleep. You must live up to your reputation as '*The Most Beautiful Face*' in the whole of England, especially on your wedding day!"

"Only one newspaper said I was the most beautiful and I don't take that too seriously. I don't care what they said and I don't care if I look hideous. I don't know what I'm doing. I think I'll get up and see if I can find James." (James was Ken's only brother who had survived the war. Since Daddy was not allowed out of Spain yet, and Piti and Ken were still in Durban, James was going to give me away at my wedding to Richard.)

"Don't talk nonsense, darling. You're not getting up. If you don't want to sleep, at least let me try."

Poor little Mummy. She had put up with my wild behavior and often she would call out at night to make sure I was home. Sometimes Gloria answered, pretending to be me. I would come home half an hour later and Gloria would make me creep into bed as she whispered, "Be quiet. You've been home some time."

I was thinking about all the fun I'd had and Gloria was stunned that I really was getting married.

I started to laugh quietly under the covers. I had gone with Richard to see Father Casey at Spanish Place. I told him that I didn't think I should become a Catholic just because the boy I was about to marry was one.

"Then we'll have your wedding in the Chapel, and, of course you won't take the Sacraments. You make great sense, but if you decide you'd like to learn about Catholicism, you could come here twice a week and one of the young priests could enlighten you on anything you want to know. You might want to join us and then again you might not want to. I hope you do."

I liked Father Casey. The young priest was a different story. I felt he'd taken his vows too soon. The poor man was not yet ready — except he was ready to be a man and enjoy the difference in our sex. Yes sex. He needed it. He was romantically inclined. I could not give him sympathy.

Mummy finally got to sleep that night. I lay awake and thought "of all the boys I'd loved before" — or thought I had. It struck me that I was a very young fake. Oh dear. I prayed that we would both be really happy and then I slept until Gloria came bursting into the room announcing that she had decided she'd like to be my one bridesmaid!

We ran out and got her a dress. I spent more time getting her ready than I did on myself.

I think if he had seen the expression on my face he might have had second thoughts!

* * *

Mummy sat by herself in the front pew — a lovely, lonely woman until in walked Ken's mother, Mrs. Burness, and sat beside her. After the ceremony, I gave her a kiss and such a grateful hug. She had suffered with the loss of her sons. I thought she was wonderful to come and hold Mummy's hand and wish me happiness.

Richard was, without a doubt, the most handsome young man. In his uniform, he certainly looked the famous movie star that he was. He looked at me and smiled. His dimples were as deep as the ocean and his eyes as blue as the sky. His dark hair was shining. Someone whispered that we looked like brother and sister! From all the information I'd got out of Mummy we might just as well have been! We were married anyway.

Of course, we didn't have a honeymoon because Richard had to rejoin his regiment, the 27th Lancers. They were stationed in the north of England awaiting orders to go to the front — to which front they were meant to go I was never allowed to be told. Wartime secrets were protected from everyone. We lived in "digs" (a rented room in a house where the owner would feed us). She was very nice and kind.

I loved Richard, but I became awfully lonely every day and would go for long cold walks. Sometimes he would get back late at night and he and his pals would have a few drinks together after the day's training. Quite a long time later, and as the war progressed, Richard's regiment was told they would not be going overseas.

Every so often, the men had to have medical examinations. It was discovered that Richard had ear trouble, and they decided to release him.

We bought a real Tudor farmhouse in Buckinghamshire, one of the prettiest counties in England. It was very old and was surrounded by a beautiful garden. We both loved it and we decided to furnish it. Richard loved old oak; I hated it. We furnished it between us — it looked like a very pretty auction room.

We were happy. For a couple of kids in war-torn England, we really loved each other and we were also good friends.

Piti, Ken and their daughter Jennifer came back. Piti didn't recognize me, I'd gone so thin. "Oh Pat, you were so beautiful."

"Well, how do I look now?" I said angrily.

"You look pretty but much too skinny —" It was an honest sister's remark.

I started eating as much as I could. You see, I had been dieting. I wanted to have a very slim figure and I got it, but at the expense of my face. Fortunately, I was young enough to put back all the weight I'd lost. I learned then that a woman's most important feature is her face. I would never let myself get really fat, but, if I put on a little too much weight, I sat on it and let my cheek bones and my eyes attract the attention.

Richard and I made a movie together called *Don't Take It To Heart*. It has only just occurred to me, as I write this, that the title could have been giving a message to the audience or to us. It could have been just an apt title for the picture.

* * *

When the picture was finished, Twentieth Century Fox sent for Richard to return and complete his contract. I was miserable. I didn't want to go to Hollywood at all — but after all, I knew *who* I was marrying even if I didn't know much else about him.

So, with all my family to see me off, we boarded a Liberty Ship for New York. My mother's last words to me were: "Try not to tell the American directors how to direct, darling."

We had unbelievable weather and ran into the same horrendous storm that Churchill ran into going the other way. It ended up taking us 14 days to get from Southampton to New York.

We were on the ship with only two other passengers, as I recall. One was an American

My parents assured me that there was no incest in our family—so why do I appear to be in love with my look-alike.

General and the other one was, I think, an American major. Of course, there was the Captain, and there must have been a crew. The Captain reminded me of Popeye — and that's about as much as I can say, for he was consistently drunk for 14 days.

One night, the American General took charge of the situation. We heard very loud voices outside our cabin. "You are completely incapable, and I am taking over this ship."

I opened our door just a crack and I saw that Popeye was on his hands and knees. He was very, very drunk.

I thought we would never reach American shores. Well, was it my fault for not wanting to leave England?

When I closed the door, I looked at Richard and we both started to laugh. "Do you think we'll ever get there?" said I.

"Are you frightened?" he asked.

"No."

Then he put his arms round me and said, "That's all that matters. But whether we make it or not, I think we'll be all right."

I realized that we really were just getting to know each other — and we both could laugh and hope.

One of my favorite pictures.

- 3 -

California Here We Come

We continued our seemingly interminable journey through the rough seas with the Army in control. Popeye was invisible until we arrived in New York and smashed right into the dock. It had been an awful trip and it ended not with a whimper but a bang, which I suppose led me to believe that I was a big hit the moment I arrived in the United States. I had a couple of rings that were put in the safe when we boarded. I went up to ask Popeye if he could please give me back my rings. Popeye had forgotten the combination and was just about to be arrested. About three hours were spent with the American General and the police, as Popeye was now lying on his back trying to think of the combination so that I could get my jewelry. We finally did get it, and we proceeded to rush through New York so fast I scarcely saw it. They were awaiting my husband in Hollywood.

We went by train to California and I remember how beautiful it was. I saw the sunshine and I thought, "Oh what a pity the people probably won't like me. They'd tease my accent." I shivered as I thought this, and I prepared myself for a rude awakening. How wrong I was, dear God, how very wrong. California is beautiful, and the people are the nicest people I have ever met. They greeted me with open arms and were absolutely delightful. It should have occurred to me that they all loved Richard, and he was thoroughly English!

* * *

Los Angeles is unremarkable as a city but it is filled with talent, music — all the arts. People work in Los Angeles, and where people work it is far more interesting. It isn't a very pretty city, it is a city filled with culture. It has become more so all the years that I have been here.

We were met at the station by Fox's P.R. people, who drove us to the Bel Air Hotel. I got a tremendous headache. I think the sunshine was too much of a shock after all the rain in England. It certainly didn't rain constantly, but the "light" was completely different. California's light was bright and strong and I had to get used to it.

I began to wonder what my new life would be like. I would have to drive a car here. I had tried a year ago when we were going to meet my mother and father and young sister at Uxbridge Station. We were staying with Piti and Ken at the time in one of their vast estates. I asked Richard if I could drive a little. He wasn't keen on the idea, knowing that I knew practically nothing about motor cars and this one was hired from Godfrey Davis, the well known rental firm in England. "Oh, don't be silly. I'll never learn if you don't let me try."

He gave in reluctantly. So I drove proudly along a country lane. As we were getting nearer to the station, I became bolder. I wanted to "show off" in front of my parents. The Salvation Army Band was playing "Lead Kindly Light" outside the station. I couldn't find the brake so I drove straight into the Salvation Army Band. Thank God the people were all right, but their instruments were totalled, and the crash certainly did not improve the look of the Godfrey Davis' motor car.

Richard had to pretend (to his chagrin) that he'd been driving, as I hadn't got a license. He also had to replace all the musical instruments, and he was never allowed to hire another car from Godfrey Davis. He remembered that incident for a long time!

Well! I'd certainly have to learn to drive in this huge country. But I put driving out of my mind, and while Richard went to Fox, I decided to take a nap, close the shades and keep the bright sun out of my eyes. I couldn't do that for long because a gentleman named Harry Friedman who handled M.G.M. for M.C.A. (the largest agency in Hollywood) called me and said that the casting director at M.G.M. had telephoned him and said that someone in that studio wished to meet with me. I told him that I had a headache. I really didn't need to take a trip to meet someone at M.G.M. I told him to postpone it for a week or two, or better still, why didn't whoever wanted to meet me come to the hotel. He hastily said they didn't do business that way here, that I was too *laid-back* for an actress, and that I certainly should be more aggressive.

* * *

He called again the next day, apologetically. This went on until I finally agreed to let him pick me up and take me to the studio, which he did.

When we arrived at the studio, we went to the casting director's office. A. Mr. Grady was in the office. Mr. Friedman said airily, "Well, I've got Miss Medina, who is it that wants to talk to her?"

"Louis B. Mayer," was his reply.

Harry Friedman looked stunned. I didn't really understand why.

We were escorted to the executive building and up to Mr. Mayer's office. It took me a long time to find him, so long was his office, so large was his desk, and in comparison, so small was Mr. Mayer.

What he lacked in height he made up for in charm. He stood up, held out his hand and said, "Welcome to M.G.M."

I shook his hand and took a seat. That way both Mr. Mayer and Harry Friedman, standing, looked larger.

"Will you trust yourself to M.G.M.?" said the head of the studio. On his desk was a blow-up of my arrival picture. Rather good I thought.

Harry Friedman said timorously, "Do you want to make a test of her?"

"No, I don't need a test. I can sense stardom. She has it. I have only felt like this with two other people. One was Greer Garson and the other was Mickey Rooney."

No one spoke. Then Harry asked Mr. Mayer if he could sit down. He did not add, "before I fall down."

I pondered Louis B. Mayer's statement and although I have always admired Greer Garson, to be compared to Mickey Rooney was the most accurate comparison. I still feel that to be so.

"Would you sign a straight 3-year contract with this studio?"

"That sounds very nice, may I think about it?" I walked up to his desk and shook his hand.

"Certainly you may, I know what you'll decide."

I smiled, showing all my teeth, Mickey Rooney style. Then I almost lifted Harry out of his chair and dragged him the length of the office and out of the door.

Louis B. Mayer, head of Metro Goldwyn Mayer studios.

Louis B. Mayer had left MGM, apparently during an attack of amnesia. My first "star" part was a silent bit, sent to me directly by the casting director. My reaction was not silent!

- 4 -

Problems, Problems, Problems

I thought about it for a long time and then I did sign for three straight years with M.G.M. I sat at home for quite some months collecting my weekly salary and awaiting my big break.

One day, Mr. Grady telephoned me: "Do you realize how long you've been under contract to this studio and, to my knowledge, you haven't put in an appearance once?!"

"I've been waiting for a script to be presented to me," I retorted.

"Well, one's on its way now."

I was delighted until it arrived. The part I was offered was described thus: "A girl with huge eyes moves the curtain and opens the window" . . . *end of part*. No name. No dialogue.

I took a taxi and dashed to Mr. Grady's office. I was furious, "How dare you send me this bit. Mr. Mayer promised me star parts."

"Unfortunately, Mr. Mayer is no longer with us. Now you've been drawing a salary every week. If indeed he did offer you star parts, why didn't your agent get a first picture agreement?"

"I don't know what you mean, but I simply refuse to do this." I flung the script on his desk.

"The only way to refuse to perform in a picture is to talk to Benny Thau."

"Where is this Mr. Thau?"

"In the executive building."

Back to the executive building I did go. After telling Mr. Thau's secretary to announce me, I must have waited at least two hours. Many people went in and out of his office, and I sat in my chair working up a steam. The secretary said, "You can go in now."

I burst into his office. Mr. Thau's office was smaller than Mr. Mayer's, as was Mr. Thau.

"Do you realize how long you've kept me waiting?" I said.

"Miss — whatever your name is — have you heard of an actress named Joan Crawford?"

"Of course I have."

"Do you know how long Joan Crawford waited outside offices?"

"Miss Crawford, no doubt, has done a great many things I wouldn't do."

He waited to see if there was more.

"What is your name and why do you want to see me?"

I told him my plight.

"Nobody knows you're under contract here. Have you tried to see some directors, get hold of some scripts and suggest yourself for a part?"

"Of course not, that would be most impertinent."

He laughed. Then he came over to me, too close to me. I moved, he followed.

"Are you going to chase me around the desk?"

He stopped and said quite nicely, for him, "You're too scared and I'm too tired."

"Do I have to do that bit part?"

"No," he said kindly. "But you go on Stage 7. Gene Kelly is working on *The Three Musketeers* there and George Sidney is directing. There's quite a cute part I think you could play. It's not a starring part, Miss Medina, but it's not a silent bit. Tell Gene I sent you.

I dashed out and silently entered Stage 7 where Gene Kelly had already heard from Benny Thau. Gene was an angel. I played the part of Kitty, a little maid. He helped me, and I have been a fan ever since. Lana Turner was the star.

A few nights before I started my part in *The Three Musketeers,* I was at a party at Romanoffs. Lana Turner made a marvelous "star" entrance. She was beautiful and glamorous.

She spotted me and loudly announced to all and sundry, "Patricia Medina, I've seen your wardrobe tests. They're wonderful. I'm so looking forward to working with you."

I was overcome by the public generosity of this famous star. I had long been a fan of hers.

When I started working with her, I was indeed confused to find that my scenes were played with her "stand in" and I never met her once during the entire picture. Her dressing room was next to mine. She played music constantly in between flouncing onto the set to play her scenes (with my stand in, I suppose). What a disappointment. It would not have upset me except for the noticeable display of charm she manifested at the party.

However, I was wondrously rewarded in a movie called *The Secret Heart.* I met the kindest and most superb movie star I ever worked with. Her name, Claudette Colbert.

We rehearsed for several days before shooting started. At every rehearsal, I would say, "Good morning, Ms. Colbert," and she would give me her radiant smile and would draw me into the group of actors with her arm around me.

On the day we started shooting, I went to the hairdresser and the make-up department to be apparently "done over" for the camera. It took quite a while and the make-up man found

a

a) PMC with June Allyson during a coffee break.
b) The beautiful Lana Turner.
c) Claudette Colbert having given sound, strong advice to the newcomer.

b

c

my features needed a lot of correction. This was a revelation. I had no idea I was such a problem: my eyes were too big; also, my mouth; and, my cheek bones too noticeable. Evidently, my nose was perfect!

He was charming and I walked onto the set feeling secure with my newly-arranged face.

Seeing the star of the picture, my friend Claudette, I said, "Good morning, Miss Colbert."

She opened her marvelous eyes, glared at me and said, "Who the *fuck* are you?!"

Stunned, I said, "I'm Patricia Medina. You've seen me every day."

"What have you done to your face? I thought you were so pretty."

"The make-up man has helped me to look good for the camera. He was very nice and tried so hard."

"I'll bet he did. Come in here, kid."

I followed her into her dressing room on the set.

She said softly, "Patricia, do you want to be a 'star' in the make-up room or up there on the screen?"

"Well," I said, but got no further.

"You look like hell. Go and wash your face and put your normal makeup on like yesterday."

"Oh, the make-up man will be so upset."

"So he damn well should be. Patricia, I have fought to be myself and it has paid off. It could with you. Now get out of here and don't come back looking like Margaret O'Brien. She's a brilliant child and that's her natural look. They try to paint that face on every newcomer. You're a young woman with a lovely face. Get out of here and don't come back until you look like yourself."

In fear, I washed my face and put my natural makeup on.

Later, they were shooting a close-up on Claudette over my shoulder. Suddenly, she announced, "It's six o'clock. That's the contractual time. I have to leave."

The director pleaded, "Oh, just two minutes. Just give us two minutes and you can go."

"Hell no," she said. "Two minutes tonight and tomorrow it will be five. No. I'm through."

"Please, Claudette. Just one close-up. The lighting is set."

"You damn fools. People have seen this face of mine for years. Have any of you seen the face that I'm looking at?" (She was pointing at me.) "Move the camera over here and photograph her. Good night." And she marched off the set.

So generous was she that she tried her best to help a newcomer. I gazed at her with admiration as she walked off the set with her marvelous legs in evidence, saying, "It's one minute past my contract time!"

Sometime later. I had made quite a few films, always doing my own makeup and my long black hair was loosely combed. I really thought I was learning.

I was invited to a large party. It may have been at the Goetz's. I was playing my first "bad girl" part and I had had my hair dyed a bright red.

Among the guests was Claudette. She turned round and said, "Good God! Is this Red Skelton?" Then recognizing me, "Oh, no! You've done it again. I give up. You'll never learn."

I smiled. I should have known she wouldn't let me down. "I have my hair this color for a movie."

"Now you really have me scared. What the hell kind of movies are you doing?" she stormed.

"Well, actually, I'm playing a sort of whore."

"Oh well, Patricia, you've finally got it right. Boy, do you look the part."

I never had red hair again.

Oh, Claudette, you were divine. A mixture of a sailor and a duchess. You taught me so much. There'll never be another one like you.

* * *

Richard was working. I was at home a lot since I never did learn the art of finding scripts and visiting directors I did not know, and who didn't know me. I did, however, realize it was very careless of Harry Friedman not to get a first picture in my contract, especially as I was signed up by Mr. Mayer, the most important man in the industry.

The studio telephoned me. They were testing a young man they were considering putting under contract and asked me to play a scene with him. I remember it was a scene from "Gone With The Wind." I enjoyed doing it thoroughly, although naturally, the camera was mostly on him. I don't know whether he was signed or not, but Harry Cohn, the head of Columbia Pictures, had taken a look at the test. He called my agent and said something like, "I'm interested in the girl. I sense stardom!!"

Not again! His intention was that once I was out of my contract with M.G.M., I could take over Rita Hayworth's roles. She was leaving the studio.

One evening he called me and told me to get my agent to free me from M.G.M. and Columbia would really give me the star treatment. I was ecstatic — until Harry Friedman told me that I would have to get my release from M.G.M.

"How?" I cried.

"Go to Benny Thau."

Oh no, not him! The thought of sitting outside his office again made me ill. The thought of going inside made me feel worse.

Dressed to kill, and murder was not entirely out of the question, I announced myself to his secretary. Mr. Thau immediately opened the door and said, "Come on in, honey. Now what can I do for you?"

"I would like M.G.M. to release me."

His expression changed. "Why," he said coldly.

"Well, I'm not doing anything for M.G.M. This studio is obviously not interested in me. It seems not only fair, but sensible."

He looked quite angry and repeated, "Why?"

"Columbia wants to sign me up and put me to work," I replied with complete honesty.

"I'll have to bring it up at the board meeting. I cannot decide this alone."

It was my turn to say, "Why?"

"I said I'd bring it up at the board meeting." He stood up. I was dismissed.

The board said, "No!"

Harry Cohn's next phone call to me was awful. He called me every name under the sun . . . except Patricia.

M.G.M. had refused to let me go. Instead, Columbia signed Kim Novak and she had a flourishing career.

Meanwhile, Richard was unhappy at Fox. He asked for and received his release.

I'm afraid the unhappiness had crept into our home life. We were both so young. We were a nice, handsome couple who should have been brother and sister. We looked alike, and we liked each other a lot.

Richard had had quite some experience before marrying me. I had had none. I was a sophisticated virgin, a noisy introvert. Though he was not lacking in humor himself, my crazy sense of humor jarred him. We had little quarrels, and were happier in the company of others than when we were alone.

So the breach began. Richard accepted an independent movie on the island of Capri. M.G.M. loaned me out to Fox for an undistinguished movie called *Moss Rose*. Darryl Zanuck gave me this part instead of a leading part, and I would have been perfect for saying, "Why the hell should I make a star for M.G.M.?" Or clearer words than that. Then I was loaned for a part, also in Italy, but on the Island of Ischia.

Richard working on Capri.

I, on Ischia, with the Bay of Naples between us.

It was this separation from each other that started the collapse of our marriage.

He made a great effort and managed to get some friends to bring him on their yacht to what I referred to as *my* island.

When he landed, I greeted him with a shy peck on the cheek. We went to my hotel and had lunch.

He hurried lunch and said, "Aren't you going to show me your room?"

He said it rather heartily and I knew he was nervous. For no reason I can think of, I was embarrassed when I introduced him to the cast and the director. As we started up the stairs, all eyes were on us.

They all knew *why* we were going upstairs. I was glad they didn't applaud, but they would have thought us insane if we had done anything else.

After all, he was my husband, yet, to me it felt somehow immoral — immoral but without the excitement. We were trying too hard.

Before coming to Italy, our parting had happened in the midst of a quarrel. We were both aware of that, and so we tried even harder. We tried to be worldly, tried to know each other better than we did, when what we should have done was behave like the youngsters we were and enjoy each other physically. But, as I have said, we were trying, trying to be sophisticated, trying to love more than we were able.

If I had known better, I would have realized that love, or even a strong attraction, just happens — trying is the beginning of the end. Poor Richard. He was so handsome. All the women fell for him and he had to fall in love and marry an unexcitable, embarrassed "lame duck," and he was too scared of my reaction to talk about it and help me.

When he left, I was sad and I was glad. He probably felt the same way because quite soon after that he became involved with a far more experienced girl, Nancy Oakes. (At that time, we were all girls.) Nancy was really in love with him. In my opinion, he should have married her. Try as I may, he would not give me a divorce.

* * *

We both returned to California. I moved out of the house. Much, much later, he finally signed the divorce papers. Since I had no intention of remarrying, I had a California divorce which took a year.

Now my contract was finally up at M.G.M. I had not been able to take advantage of

Louis B. Mayer's offer before he left the studio. And now Harry Cohn was gone too, never having forgiven me.

What was I to do? Out of the blue, Columbia offered me a film with Louis Hayward.

Louis was making a comeback and filming all the films that Errol Flynn and Olivia de Havilland had made. I was to play the de Havilland parts. Louis was an excellent actor. We worked well and happily together.

With Louis Hayward—happy actors.

- 5 -

Charlie Chaplin Is A Girl

Louis and I were friendly, but we never discussed our private lives. We made at least four movies together. I do remember clearly that in one of our pictures I had to disguise myself as a boy — actually, I was a princess and Louis was in love with me. To get into his cabin on the ship, I had to dress up as a cabin boy.

Louis was not working on the day I had to try on my wardrobe. First, with a pair of pants, I wore a very loose jacket to conceal my most unboyish figure. I washed my face so it was devoid of any makeup. Lastly, I pulled up my long black hair and tucked it into a big Jackie Coogan-like cap. In fact, with no makeup and my hair under that marvelous cap, I did look a little like Jackie Coogan. I paraded myself in front of the producer, Eugene Frenke.

Frenke looked at me for a long time and then in utter disgust, he said, "You don't look like a boy."

"Well, Louis discovers I'm not a boy and we have our final love scene."

He seemed not to have heard me.

"Your ears are not like a boys, it just won't do."

I was fed up and I turned on him and said, disdainfully, "What do you want me to do, wear a moustache?"

"Marvelous idea," said Frenke. I was, for once, speechless.

I finally had to submit to his judgement and was driven to the Max Factor Salon.

When I saw Bob Roberts, whom I'd known for a long time, he looked at me in amazement. "Patricia, tell me it isn't true that I have to put a moustache on you." He was almost in tears.

"That's what the producer wants, so give me a nice Ronald Colman moustache!"

Poor Bob glued on a dear little moustache and I was driven to the studio scaring people at stop lights. I was greeted by a delighted producer.

"That's just what you needed, I'll see you tomorrow," slapping me gently on the buttocks (today it could be said he harassed me). He was gone.

Looking at myself in the mirror, I appeared more like Charlie Chaplin than Coogan. I looked around for a little Chaplin walking stick. Not finding one, I went home to get some rest before my big scene.

That night, Louis telephoned me. He had never telephoned me before, so I realized it must be important.

"I've just heard that Frenke has asked you to wear a moustache, it can't be true."

I told him it was and gave him the whole story.

"I'm not going to kiss a girl who wears a moustache and that's that. Patricia, you don't want to ruin our last scene, do you?"

I assured him I thought the whole idea was dreadful and I knew he'd be ready for the fight with Frenke in the morning.

When I arrived, there was no one to be seen. So I went and dressed, washed my face and suffered through the spirit gum that stuck on the moustache.

I walked on the set to the sound of loud voices.

Louis: "Don't you know I realize that she's not a boy. I take off her cap and as her hair falls to her shoulders we kiss. That's the way to play it."

"When you take off her cap and her hair falls down, you take off her moustache and you kiss," yelled Frenke.

Quietly, I walked to Louis' side, looked up at him and twitched my moustache. The horror on his face sent me into gales of laughter. Frenke was furious as I knew he would be.

And then Louis pulled the trigger. He walked off the picture. "Get another actor," he said as he stormed off the set.

I waited quietly until I heard Louis' footsteps returning. He was triumphant. Without a word, I painfully removed the moustache and washed my face.

We proceeded with the film sans moustache as if there had been no interruption.

This was the picture that had Walter Wanger as the executive producer. Walter was an elegant gentleman, he would come daily to the set in his immaculate suit, sporting a red carnation.

Sometime into the movie, there was a much-publicized interruption. Walter believed that his wife (the beautiful Joan Bennett) was being unfaithful with her agent, so he unsuccessfully shot the gentleman in question and was arrested.

While doing a scene with Louis, I saw Walter standing at the entrance to the set dressed as usual, but what was noticeably missing was his red carnation. Everyone was silent, except when I heard myself saying too clearly, "Walter, what else is new?" Walter did not reply but turned and walked into my dressing room and sat down.

After we shot the scene, I followed him and looked at him. I felt embarrassed and sad, so I just asked, "Why did you do it?"

He gave me a triumphant smile and said, seriously, "I got Eisenhower off the front page."

Obviously, this was a case of temporary insanity. A misfortune for those concerned.

Although Joan Bennett is reputed to have rushed round to her former husband, writer-producer Gene Markey, and, as he went to console her, she said, "If only you had shot Walter this would never have happened." Mr. Markey told me this story himself!

Poor Walter paid a price, and was, I believe, "put away for a while." Sanity must have returned as he produced several movies later on.

There was no need for him to wear a crown, he was the king. He also happened to be the number one star in Hollywood.

- 6 -

The King, the Lover and that Face

The picture finished; Louis and I parted happily. We would meet the next time on another set. I was now working consistently and had become a very able actress. One thing I had to decide: I had either to hire a chauffeur, take a million busses or learn to drive. I chose the latter and got my permit, but I had to drive with someone else until I took my test.

My good friend, Carl Esmond's wife, Ruthie, volunteered for this hazardous task. (Carl was a big star in Vienna. He escaped Hitler and acted in England, then made many movies in the United States.) Universal Studios, where I was preparing to make a picture with Donald O'Connor, brought a gentleman from the DMV over to take me for my test.

After driving for what seemed like ages, I returned with speed to the studio and came to a screeching halt. The gentleman left the car mopping his brow with trembling hands. A voice said, "Miss Medina, I'm going to give you a license because I definitely think you should drive alone!"

Now I could act and I could drive . . . perilously. I ran into my instructor (not with my car) on the lot a few weeks later. He said, "Have you learned how to park correctly?"

"No," I replied somewhat shyly. "But you see, I've been quite clever really. I find the places I go to have parking gentlemen (valet parking). It's quite an art; I do watch them sometimes."

"It's been very nice knowing you, Miss Medina." As he said it he smiled, but I couldn't help thinking that this was "goodbye" and possibly "good riddance!"

* * *

Richard and I made several attempts at resuming our life together, but they were unsuccessful, and we had to let the divorce proceed.

A divorce is a sad thing, especially when both people like each other very much. My family was upset. This was the first pending divorce in our family.

My mother came out to be with me. Richard had greeted her in New York with flowers and a wish that she could talk me out of my decision. She did not. Although her company was a great comfort, I told her that our marriage was far from perfect. She stayed with me for a few weeks. I saw her off at the station on her way to New York and then she flew to England. When she arrived home, she wrote me a lovely letter saying that as she rode off in the train, she cried because she thought when she left me I looked so small and lost and she wished I had someone to look after me. I didn't need anyone except friends, and Richard was certainly a friend, and a friend he remained for the rest of his life until he died some years ago.

In between pictures, I had a very stimulating social life. I did have many friends, like Carl Esmond and his brave wife Ruthie (who had risked her life when I was learning to drive). David Selznick and his beautiful wife Jennifer Jones, who invited me often to their house, and I loved going there, where the people I met were always lively, humorous and intellectual. I would drive perilously to whatever house they were entertaining in and would drive home carefree, stimulated and happy.

* * *

I spent most Sundays at Mary Lee and Douglas Fairbanks Jr.'s. A group was invited to swim and have tea and then stay on for spaghetti dinners. Some people just came for dinner.

In the afternoon, I saw quite a few people swimming beautifully, and "show off" that I was, I jumped into the pool. After doing half a length, I was going down for the third time. I waved my hands and tried to cry for help. Douglas Fairbanks Jr. came and rescued me. I have to give him his full name and full credit for saving my life. He said for a second he thought I was joking but didn't take a chance. Thank God and Douglas.

I enjoyed dinners with them very much because they were very casual and we all just sat where we liked.

The first evening that I was invited, I helped myself to spaghetti, with all the others — I spotted an empty table and sat down with my dinner. A gentleman came and sat down beside me. I looked at him. It was Clark Gable. That was the first time that I had met him.

A rather boring gentleman sat on my other side and his wife sat beside him. Out of nowhere, he turned to me and said, "Do you like children?"

I said, "Yes, I do, but I don't have any."

"How lucky you are," was his response. Then, "My wife and I didn't want any children, but I guess we didn't handle it very well because look what we had by accident."

He handed me a photo of five of the ugliest children I have ever seen. One was sticking out his tongue, one was squinting, and the others were all pulling faces.

I was quite alarmed by this sudden presentation and could think of nothing else to do but to hand the photo to Mr. Gable as I said, "Look what they had by accident."

He was taking a gulp of wine and choked on it.

I had such fun with him. I didn't see him as the screen lover. We just took off right away as friends — as fun friends. I didn't think of him as "The King" until the second time we met.

David Niven and his wife Hjordis gave a dinner party at Romanoff's Restaurant. It was the "in" place at the time — and "in" we all were, for David had chosen to have a long table in the back room right up against the wall. All of us with our backs to the wall faced the room — rather like the *Last Supper.*

After the first course, I began to feel very uncomfortable. Gable, who was sitting next to me, said, "Patricia, why are you looking nervous?"

"I have a problem," I said, quickly.

He raised his eyebrows and twinkled at me wickedly. "Want to tell me?"

"I have to go to the ladies' room."

"And how do you propose to manage that stunt?"

Without answering him, I slipped down underneath the table and crawled out the other side. I stood up and someone took my arm. It was Clark.

He had done exactly as I had and came up from under the table beside me. We didn't say a word — but, taking my arm, he walked me through the entire restaurant to the ladies' room. All eyes were upon us.

When I came out, he was waiting at the door, took my arm again and we silently retraced our steps to the back room under the table and took our seats.

Oh, yes, he was The King.

* * *

Sam Goldwyn (the Dean of Hollywood) and his wife Francis included me in their dinner parties and we would always watch a movie after dinner — Mr. Goldwyn was no longer producing pictures.

One evening at their house, he walked over to me and said, "I saw you in a movie the other day. You have talent."

I was thrilled and mumbled, "Thank you, Mr. Goldwyn."

"You are making one big mistake."

Oh God, what could that be?

"Patricia, you should go blonde."

I was stunned. "Mr. Goldwyn, my eyes are almost black, whatever would I look like blonde?"

"Very nice, I think. You see, dear, you are a comedienne, you are never going to get comedy roles with that black hair. You are always going to be a heavy or a vamp, a bad girl. Blonde — I see you as a second Carole Lombard."

Having said his piece, he walked off and talked to someone else.

All these years later, I ponder and wonder why I didn't become a bigger star. Forget M.G.M. letting me down. Forget Harry Cohn. I had been given the best advice from the Dean of Hollywood and did not take it. The only blame was mine, my stupidity. Since the start I had always wanted to play comedy parts, and not until many years later and on the stage did I play comedy successfully. In movies, I was never offered anything but sexy bad girls. Let me not say that I didn't enjoy them, but Mr. Goldwyn, why were you such a gentleman? Why didn't you hit me on my stupid, stubborn black head?

* * *

I have spoken about my unsuccessful marriage. I have mentioned that I was entertained socially in between pictures, how I didn't need to be looked after. Real love had eluded me. Oh, how untruthful I have been, I have become very Americanized since I left England but I really existed on the love for and from my family. There was not a Christmas that I didn't go to England. Sometimes arriving on December 24th. At London airport they would all be there: Mummy, Daddy, Piti and Ken. Gloria and her husband Gerry. The press would greet me as I got off the plane and they would say, "They're all here!" and they seemed as excited as I was.

Every success I had, I called and shared with them, all my loneliness, and yes, I was indeed at times very lonely. I called upon their company over the telephone, to tell them how I missed them and to hear of their need for me. My parents came several times to be with me. But at Christmas, no matter what was going on in my life, I flew home to celebrate, even for just a week.

Robert Sherr, my agent at Famous Artists Agency, called me and told me I was offered a movie with John Wayne. The part — a little Mexican girl (very suited to my dark eyes and black hair and my Spanish blood).

"When does it go?" I asked.

"Starts December 16th."

"Impossible," I said. "You know I have to go home."

"Patricia, this is John Wayne. You can go home when you're finished."

"They wouldn't understand," I said softly.

I did not make the picture. I went home and I saw them all waiting at the airport. As my mother embraced me, I said, "Mummy, I was offered a picture with John Wayne, but I refused it. I said you wouldn't understand if I didn't come home for Christmas."

"Darling," she said, "I certainly would not have understood it."

Well, I had guessed one thing correctly. And that Christmas was more wonderful than any movie.

So back and forth I went.

* * *

I did enjoy one romance with a very attractive man. He was single. I was separated. We enjoyed each other to the fullest. Neither of us was ready for marriage. He because he was scared, maybe of me. I because my dreams of marriage had been shattered. I had expected perfection.

The relationship lasted quite a while. We fought constantly and made up at great lengths.

I suppose we could have been referred to as "going unsteady."

I remember his car had no heater. If it had, it didn't work, so he gallantly put a small portable heater on my side of the car. It got so hot I don't know why it didn't set fire to the car. One day it simply petered out (unfortunate word, but I am referring to the heater).

John Wayne, the Duke. I wish I'd had a second chance to work with him.

When our romance (good word this time) was over, I wondered if the heater hadn't been responsible for the whole thing — the warmth, the comfort, hence the passion which I had never known before. Whatever the cause, I do not regret the experience. Contrary to my upbringing, I wasn't in the least ashamed of having had a love affair. In fact, I was glad to discover I was not a cold English woman. Now I could live my life unattached forever.

As the man said, "It ain't over till it's over." So, when it was over, I had my work, I had my family, I had been married and I had been bedded by a lover. They both had been decent men.

* * *

So, back to work. As I had so improperly said to Walter Wanger — "What else is new?"

Paramount offered me a picture with Alan Ladd called *Botany Bay.* It was a good picture and though, of course, I played a bad girl, I enjoyed it very much.

Apparently, I was not the first choice for the part. Joan Fontaine, under contract to Paramount, was who they really wanted for the picture. She was an expensive actress and so was the picture. They had to decide whether to make the picture in black and white with

a

b

a) James Mason. Always gave a fine performance. He was born to act.
b) Alan Ladd, James Mason and the "Bad" girl in Botany Bay.
b) Donald O'Connor and two friends in the first Francis.

c

Joan (a proven box office attraction and a fine actress), or to make the picture in Technicolor with a less expensive actress. Since Alan Ladd was a highly expensive box office attraction and James Mason, who was also in the picture, was surely costing them plenty, Paramount decided to go with two male stars and a less expensive actress — me, as the leading lady.

Working with James was a joy. He was secure in his talent and personality, and he brought out the best in anyone who was playing a scene with him. Luckily, we had many scenes together.

Working with Alan was different. He was a star. Every close up told a story. They say certain actors made love to the camera. In Alan's case the camera made love to him. He was shy, introverted, almost ashamed of being a top-notch actor, but regardless of with whom Alan was playing a scene, the camera seemed to seek him out (without instructions or demands from Alan) and kiss him so that he jumped onto the screen and all the elements appeared to be whispering, "Star, star!"

He seemed totally unaware of this. Much has been made about his lack of height and he seemed in person, I suppose, quite a small man. But on the screen, he was huge.

I felt he didn't really care for stardom, as he was shy about mixing with other actors and preferred being with the crew. He had begun his career as a gaffer, before being discovered by agent Sue Carrol, who later became his wife.

He probably needed more confidence. The fact that his natural talent flowed out of him, but did not feed his ego. It was heavily undernourished.

On the next picture I made with him, he loosened up a bit. We never became close friends, like I had with James Mason, or Louis Hayward, or Donald O'Connor, but I was very proud to have played opposite him. I liked him very much.

* * *

Universal Studios started out being very strange for me. The movies I made there were cheap, and I was supporting some very funny fellows.

I made a movie called *Abbott and Costello in the Foreign Legion.* I was warned that they would give me a hard time and play jokes on me. They were perfect little gentlemen and treated me with great respect. I played a very sexy French spy.

Then, with Donald in the first *Francis,* I played — *a sexy French spy.*

Thinking back, I played very few English parts. Whatever nationality, Universal became like home to me.

The first day on one of those pictures, I walked into the commissary for lunch, and it was absolutely crowded. Not a seat to be had.

A tall, wonderful-looking gentleman at the very end of the room waved to me, then beckoned me over to his table.

"Sit here," said Cary Grant.

I looked directly at that face and sat down. If there hadn't been a chair there I still would have sat. What a charming, splendid-looking man. He never received an award, but he was a superb actor. Those were the days when they thought "comedy" was easy! A stupid decision.

Lunching every day with Cary Grant, the food was unimportant. It was difficult to stop gazing at that face. Tall, dark and handsome was an understatement.

From that day until the end of my picture, I would walk into the commissary and Cary would stand and hold the chair which I flopped in. We would have stimulating conversations: serious ones, funny ones, quiet ones — *until* one dreadful day, we had a disagreement.

We were talking about our childhoods and parents and beliefs. Cary said, "I think it quite wrong that children are taught to believe in Santa Claus. It's lying. Lying to children from the start." He continued quite heatedly about how wrong children were brought up.

I strongly disagreed with him. I told him I had believed in Santa and when I discovered it was my father, I was older, and laughed and never felt I had been lied to.

He turned on me and said, "Well, it's easy for you to talk with your ritzy upbringing. Everything had to be invented if you were poor. *You* were brought up in the lap of luxury, so you only see one side."

This unhappy discussion proceeded until it was time for me to leave and go back to work on the picture.

We were working on the back lot. So, as I walked back, I stopped at the little shop next to the commissary to buy some mints. I saw a rack with cards and flicked it around. I found a card. The cover was a silver shoe and inside it said:

"Can I help it if I was born with a silver foot in my mouth?"

I bought it, signed it "Patricia" and asked one of the pages to deliver it to Mr. Grant's office.

About an hour later, a big chauffeur-driven Rolls Royce drove up to the back lot. The chauffeur got out. He was holding an envelope. He came and handed it to me saying, "Miss Medina, Mr. Grant asked me to give you this."

I opened the letter. It was on his bold stationery. He wrote, "Darling, Please forgive me. I love you. (signed) Santa Claus, P.S. Will you marry me?"

* * *

We were friends again. Good friends. (No, I did not have an affair with him.) Beautiful though he was, I felt real friendship and admiration for him. I never thought of him as a lover — and we know I would never marry again, don't we?

Anyway, to be perfectly honest, I think he was very apprehensive about my "silver foot." He thought I was a funny, pretty "snob", I'm sure, though we stayed clear of the subject. I think he was in love with Sophia Loren.

Some houses can be homes, some homes can be houses. Few can be both.

- 7 -

Allah Be Praised

I moved into a bungalow at the Garden of Allah. It was a famous building — infamous really — for the interesting brilliant people who had left their colorful and black marks there.

I discovered that this place I decided to live in had quite a history. It was originally owned by silent screen star Alla Nazimova and opened in 1926 amid orange groves. It had twenty-five bungalows which were inhabited by more celebrities than any other place in Hollywood, such as Gloria Swanson, Rudolph Valentino, Marlene Dietrich, the Barrymores, Greta Garbo, etc.

Scott Fitzgerald lived there while romancing Sheilah Graham; Robert Benchley lived there; and, of course, Errol Flynn. All attractive, witty, lovers of women and lovers of booze.

Rumor has it that one night Robert Benchley was awakened from a whisky-induced sleep. A voice beside him asked, "Get me a glass of water." He got up slowly, staggered to the bar and returned with a glass of water to find the bed empty. The voice he had heard came from the apartment next door. The walls were notoriously thin.

I took the largest bungalow, which had belonged to Errol Flynn and was, of course, totally detached. They say the wicked Errol had trouble getting the maids to clean out his bungalow because when they bent over to make his bed he goosed them!

Those three have left tales of wild nights and excuses for hung-over mornings. It must have been really something, unfortunately, before I arrived in this country. Benchley, I believe, had the best excuse. When he was suffering from a horrendous hangover, a friend said kindly, "Maybe it was something you ate for breakfast." "No, no. It can't be that," he said, "as I always have just one aspirin for breakfast, lightly grilled." He was, it seems, a brilliant writer — for the *New Yorker, Life* and many other magazines and newspapers.

Scott Fitzgerald was unique. He needs no explanation and probably defies description, but his works will always haunt us.

As for Flynn, I wish I had met him. I don't know whether his wit compared with the others. His capacity for liquor surely did. And I imagine he broke more hearts than all of them put together. I found his bungalow comfortable and cheerful and safe. I felt it was safe because if, as I thought, the bungalows still had bad reputations, the police would surely come out immediately upon being called.

Not long after I had settled into my bungalow my agent called me and offered me two movies. One was *Valentino* and the other was *Jackpot* with Jimmy Stewart.

He said, "I'll make an appointment for you to see Eddie Small this afternoon and see if he wants you for the part of Valentino's first wife. Then you're going to have to choose between the two parts."

"I want to do *Jackpot*," I said. "Who would miss the chance of acting with Jimmy Stewart?"

"Right," said Bob. "Then I'll cancel the date with Mr. Small."

"You won't. I'd like to do both parts if it's at all possible," was my greedy retort. So off I went to see the producer of *Valentino*.

Eddie Small: "You certainly look the part, my dear, but I have never heard of you doing any dancing, and this is a very difficult and professional dance."

Patricia: "Mr. Small, I am a dancer. Maybe you've never seen me because I danced professionally in Spain."

Eddie Small: "Well, that's very, very interesting, Miss Medina. I suggest you go over to Stage 8 where Larry Ceballos, the dance instructor, is going through the routine with Antony

With Antony Dexter in Valentino. *Left profile always showing.*

Dexter and a professional dancer. You could go and try some of the steps and if Larry Ceballos says you're okay, the part is yours."

Patricia (very softly): "Thank you, Mr. Small."

Antony Dexter had been groomed by Eddie Small, not only to look like the great lover but to dance exactly like him. Under Mr. Small's tuition and with a dance instructor for three years, the result was very effective. One side of his face was pure Valentino (the left side), and his acting was passable. Since Mr. Valentino was never heard to speak, there was no way to compare his acting, so he was given the benefit of the doubt. Eleanor Parker played his lady love, and no one has criticized her acting or her looks. She is a fine and lovely actress.

So, I went down to see Mr. Ceballos at Stage 8 and was confronted with a reasonable facsimile of the great lover. He was slashing his whip loudly on the floor while the girl professional dancer was turning and twirling magnificently. He cracked the whip so fast that it flew through the air and landed round her waist, and she turned and turned letting the whip go round her, twirling directly to him until she was in his arms.

Ashen, I sat down on a stool, put my head between my legs and breathed deeply while praying.

Dexter came sidling over to me, only the left side of his face in evidence.

He lifted me up forcefully, grabbing me tightly. He gave me a passionate possessive kiss, then dropped me on my blessed stool.

He moved slowly backwards, left side of his face taking in my whole person. "Patricia," he said, "If I may call you that?" What a ridiculous question, he'd almost raped me. He continued, "Let's you and I try taking it from the top."

I walked slowly over to Larry Ceballos. After all, he was the dance instructor.

"Mr. Ceballos," I said softly. "I have just returned from doing a very dramatic scene with Jimmy Stewart" (I had done no such thing). "I do not think it would be fair to you, to Mr. Dexter or to me to jump into a dancing mood today." I don't think they cared about my mood, but I was depending on the name James Stewart to help me out. I was buying time. They decided to call it a day.

Dexter and the professional dancing girl left together. She was obviously crazy about him. Larry Ceballos stayed with me.

"Do you drink?" I asked.

"Yes," said Ceballos.

"Why don't we walk over to the Formosa, have a drink and get to know each other."

Prompt agreement.

After he'd ordered a Bloody Mary, I whispered to the barman to make it a stiff one. I dropped the bomb.

"I have never danced a step in my life," I said very clearly.

Several giant-sized drinks later, I told Larry Ceballos my plan.

I needed his help and I needed to extract a promise from him never to divulge our present conversation to anyone. I waited until he'd had several more drinks and his eyes crossed. Then, we made our deal.

The film had already started and they needed Dexter most of the time. We shot in two weeks' time. I employed a male professional dancer and we worked night and day, only stopping for Larry's refills. When it came time to shoot, Dexter grabbed me in a vise. Then he flung me with all his might cracking the whip like thunder. I called upon God, having already used Jimmy Stewart (the next best thing). What do you know?

* * *

We did that number in two takes. I had worked at Fox many days on *Jackpot* at the same time that I was working nights until midnight with the professional dancer that I employed. We kept him hidden the entire time. When I went to bed those nights, I felt like never getting up again.

But it paid off, the dance was over and I had to do his death scene with him the next day. I cried during the scene. It has always been easy for me to summon tears for a scene but this time I just sobbed because my legs were aching so much and I hated Dexter for being allowed to play the scene quietly in bed!

Meanwhile, I was enjoying making *Jackpot* with Jimmy Stewart. I played a French artist that he won in a jackpot competition. Of course, he and his wife expected the artist to be a gentleman. When I arrived at the house looking and sounding very French, of course, I played havoc with his marriage. It was a very amusing film but I think it was ahead of its time and didn't receive the success it deserved.

Valentino was released, and it was a mild success so they sent Antony Dexter and me on a personal appearance tour to hopefully boost the box office. We were accompanied by a P.R. man from the studio.

Our first appearance was in Cleveland after the matinee. I walked on stage first, still in my travelling suit. They didn't expect me to have an English accent. I was asked how I learned to dance so well. I said that I had had great teachers and that I had worked day and night. Mr. Small had guessed that my dancing professionally in Spain was a lie. So why try it on Cleveland?

We had no prepared dialogue. Some quite inept young man on the stage asked me the most boring questions. I finally interrupted him by saying to the audience, "Wouldn't you like to meet the star of the picture?"

Applause at last. On came Dexter walking slightly sideways, left side of his face to the audience. He looked like Valentino in a slept-in suit.

He was asked if he had danced as a child. He said, "No." He wasn't allowed to for fear of scaring the congregation (his father was a minister, I believe). That remark about scaring the congregation could have been quite funny except for the way he said it!

Each question got a little less romantic and the answers more sophomoric. I said, "Mr. Valentino, we're going to be late for our date. Goodbye, Ladies and Gentlemen."

I took him and the bewildered question master and dragged them off stage. About three people applauded half-heartedly.

I told the P.R. man that I was going home, that they didn't want to hear my "piss-elegant" accent, and that Tony should not be allowed to speak out of his own home.

"Don't go," pleaded the P.R. man. "Can you help us in any way?"

"The only thing I can suggest is that Tony wear tails. I have a long red chiffon evening dress. I could come on stage and say, 'Ladies and Gentlemen, would you like to meet Rudolph Valentino?' When he comes on stage, I say, 'Rudolph, would you dance with me?' We do a few steps (which we could work on in Tony's suite) and then dance, hopefully to thunderous applause."

The P.R. man thought the idea great, so we went to Tony's suite.

Obviously, expecting a maid or some fan, he opened the door sideways and stood there in the dressing gown he wore in the picture! The P.R. man told him my idea. He solemnly agreed to it. We worked out some great steps. I must say, he really could dance.

In the evening show, we wowed them. They wanted an encore. Antony was about to walk on stage.

"We don't have an encore," I hissed in a most unlady-like fashion.

"I could speak to them," he said.

Oh, dear heavens, he meant it.

The P.R. man got him by one arm, I grabbed the other and we literally pulled him to the car.

Travelling to the next town, Tony was seized with a case of laryngitis. My introduction from then on was a joy. I told them what had happened to Tony's voice so I said, "You'll have to imagine that the real silent screen star is here as Mr. Dexter is unable to speak." I did not say, "Thank heavens." The rest of the tour, though long, was uneventful but successful.

Having dinner, when in Chicago, sitting in a booth, Tony whispered to me, "You're in the wrong place."

"Oh, am I not supposed to have any dinner?" said I.

"Don't be silly," he said shyly. "You're on the wrong side. Would you change seats so I can talk to you?"

"Oh, the left side!" Poor, poor nice fellow might have a stiff neck from now on. We changed sides and as we did, it seemed to me that everyone in the Pump Room thought we were playing musical chairs.

I can't remember what town we were in but the stage manager came to me and said, "When you ask him to dance, step upstage a little and you'll have more room."

I thought he'd said to step upstage immediately, but apparently, I misunderstood him and I stepped up too soon, just as the curtains were parting. I was enfolded in those heavy, filthy things as they were drawn to the side. Tony was left on stage like a lost soul calling my name. I finally came out on my hands and knees, pitch black, from head to foot. I almost sang a chorus of "Mammy" but thought better of it.

The audience adored it and applauded so long and so loudly, that I was thinking of how to keep it in the show in other towns. I said "thinking." We were lucky. I made a mistake and it worked. The reason that it worked was that it was unintentional. But Tony stuck to the script and said his line, "Can we dance?" I was sooty from head to foot. I'm glad he said "can" instead of "shall."

I was rather sorry for him, but after he heard the applause in the theatre, he asked Eddie Small for twice the salary. I thought that ungrateful — after all, Small had paid him for three years while training for the role. He did not get the raise in salary. He made several more movies. I don't think for Eddie Small. Anyway, I have never seen him again.

Eddie Small did offer me another picture, I think it was meant to be payment for carrying on with the tour. I didn't do it. However, I have great respect for Mr. Small.

* * *

I was a little depressed after the *Valentino* saga and began to have that fear which is common to many actors. Two weeks, that seemed like two years, went by without hearing from my agent. I thought I might never work again. Then one large thick envelope arrived!

It was a script, in Italian, sent by an agent who had heard that I spoke Italian. He wrote that Napoli Films were due to start on the enclosed script starring Carlo Fuente (an Italian movie star) and they wanted me to play opposite him. It was to be shot at a studio near the port of Livorno (Leghorn) with exteriors in Portofino!

I read the script. It was quite mediocre *but* the Italian Riviera, and especially Portofino, made it seem like *Gone With The Wind*. I accepted with alacrity.

The director telephoned me to say how delighted they all were that I had agreed to do it. Arrangements were made for me to fly to Naples where they would meet me. He said he had my measurements from Columbia, my clothes were being made in Rome and sent to Naples.

Of course, it was a costume film. The only measurements they would need would be the length, waist and chest. He told me he admired my lovely large eyes.

As we landed in Naples, I was astonished at the amount of photographers approaching the plane. Who were they expecting? It couldn't be me. The only photographers that ever greeted me were the English lot, but that was because it was "Home" and nearly always at Christmas time.

A large lady, a publicity person, entered the plane and said, "Signorina Medina?"

I stood up and went to meet her.

"*Benvenuto a Italia*," she said and kissed me on both cheeks.

The moment I set foot on Italian soil, a photographer rushed up and almost broke my nose with his camera. I thought he was X-raying my sinuses. But, the following day, there was a photo in the newspaper of *my eyes!* At that time, the Italians referred to me as "*Gli Occhi*" . . . "The Eyes."

Everyone was charming. The clothes fit perfectly, so we set off for the Livorno Studios and prepared to shoot the interiors.

The different countryside and the sea air helped to make the script seem better than it was.

In Italy, a photographer took a very close painful picture of me. The next day in the newspaper there was a picture of my eyes only, hence the caption, "Gli Occhi . . . the eyes."

The studios were small but very comfortable and seemed to function efficiently. I stayed in a hotel in Livorno.

The director, the gentleman who had originally telephoned me, was in full charge of the production. He was a master with the camera, and, although the crew and the actors seemed to like him, he had a habit of screaming obscenities at the slightest mistake. To me, he was deferential and kind and was able to change from a tyrant into an attractive, helpful director. His clothes were atrocious. Although he seemed to change often, his pants were always smattered with paint.

I asked him about his choice of wardrobe.

"I am not a gentleman. I am a Communist and an artist," he said, stroking a particularly strong orange color on his pants as he dashed off to loudly scold some poor actor who indeed was most unable and having trouble with his lines which were mercifully few.

I was interested that the director was an artist. Now we could be friends. I told him I'd like to see some of his paintings. He had a studio nearby and one on the Via Margutta in Rome.

One lunch hour he took me to his local studio. It was a revelation. Mostly nudes and nearly all women, they were tastefully arranged either on sofas or chairs or standing by screens of various marvelous colors.

In his studio, he was a different person. There was no shouting; he was quiet, serious and secure, apparently in his appreciation of the female form and of rainbow hues.

I told him I had painted a lot as a girl and how much I had loved it. He asked why I had stopped and we became friends.

One day after I'd finished shooting, he told me that I didn't work the following day and that he had two tickets to a prize fight and would I like to go with him. I accepted his most unglamorous invitation really because I had nothing else to do.

The fight started with two young, agile fighters. They were fierce but quite graceful. Their fight was the first half of the program. At intermission, we both had a glass of cheap chianti, and, while drinking, he told me that he had decided to move to Portofino earlier than intended as he'd finished shooting in and around Livorno and Portofino was so much more beautiful. This delighted me.

He said all the transportation was arranged for the company, but he would take me so that I could see the approach to that haven and he could point out all the beautiful sights, and, perhaps interest me in painting again. Before I could thank him for his thoughtfulness, the second fight was announced. These were the stars. We were rushed to our seats through a noisy, excited throng.

They were aiming to kill each other. At one point, the bigger of the two knocked his opponent out of the ring and the sound of bone shattering and the sight of blood flowing terrified me. I hid my face in my new friend's shoulder and one hand reached out and touched his leg. I was unconsciously, gently stroking his leg while crying and clinging to him. The screeching was horrendous, and, when I lifted my tear-stained face, he looked long into my eyes.

Finally, he helped me up and we left. Silence . . .

Oh, dear God, had I made a careless gesture?

He took me back to my hotel, told me he'd pick me up at 8:00 A.M. "Tomorrow will be different, it will be beautiful." He kissed my hand and said, "Goodnight, Carina," and left.

Of course, all our conversation was in Italian. I went directly to bed but didn't sleep. I stayed awake thinking of my behavior at the fight. Did I intentionally stroke his leg, fling my arms around him and cry? I tried to think of the Italian word for "tease."

* * *

At 8:00 A.M., we started our journey to the Italian Riviera. Much, much later on, we stopped. No explanation needed. We were silently gazing at the most beautiful shoreline. The blue, blue Mediterranean and here and there an occasional pristine white house. Bougainvillaea poured before us, all different colors, occasionally interrupted by the cypress trees for which Italy is famous.

He started the car and stopped again at a little cafe overlooking that unrealistic ocean. We had a Campari soda and took off again. It was getting late.

There was a lavish hotel at Amalfi but we passed it and stopped at a smaller one.

"We'll break the journey here and get to Portofino in the morning when the light is best," he said.

We never mentioned the fight. He told me to wait in the car while he checked the hotel. He came out smiling. We gave our passports at the desk, took the elevator to the fifth floor, and after a short walk, he unlocked the door to a room with a view and one large bed.

"Whose room is this?" I asked.

"Ours," was the response.

I then let go in fury. I can't remember what I said but it was cold anger. I walked out of the room talking about my reputation, my name being on the passport, and ordered him to go downstairs at once and get two rooms — which he did.

When he came back, he silently handed me a key and disappeared. I was upset, never having had to cope with a situation like this. Part of my upset was guilt. I certainly *had* touched his leg. I had jumped at the idea of his bringing me on this, up to now, beautiful trip. Homesick and confused, I went into my small room, got undressed and into bed.

About half an hour later, a door opened on the left side of the bed. I had not noticed it. (He had gone down to the desk as I had ordered and changed the reservation to two rooms — *two adjoining rooms!*)

Wearing just a toweling robe, he walked past the bed to the window and looked out. I said not a word.

After a while, he came over, pulled the bed clothes off me and with one hand tore my nightdress from top to bottom. I was totally exposed to him. I did not move a muscle. I closed my eyes and awaited the dreaded rape. If he was determined to take me, I was equally determined that it would have to be just that. I would not react at all to his attack . . . *unless,* and this I truly feared, he was going to be brutal and beat me up (maybe he was sadistic and enjoyed that fight). One hit and I would scream the place down, calling for help. To hell with passports or reputation. I was not going to be violated! Nor was I.

I didn't hear him leave the room, my eyes were closed and my heart was beating too fast. I continued to lie there fully exposed. My beautiful green nightdress stayed torn at each side of my naked body. Exhausted, I went to sleep.

* * *

I was awakened by the gentlest kisses round my shoulders and throat and my breasts. I felt as if a butterfly had decided to arouse me tenderly. The kisses became faster. The butterfly was teasing me.

I didn't open my eyes but I could not stem the flow of tears from quietly covering my face.

"I should have said *yes* or *no*," I whispered. "Not *maybe*. I'm sorry."

His kisses continued. His hands were soft and hard at the same time and very experienced.

"I'd like to make you not sorry," he said. And he did.

Each time he found a new and thrilling pleasure while teaching me a world I had never known, he would whisper, "I love you." Somehow, I simply could not return that phrase.

I learned, with apparent ease, every way in which to receive and to give my lustful need, and I discovered that "going to bed" was not the only way to consummate passion. Oh, no! The floor, the walls, the shower. It all seemed to me to be necessary, unceasing and complete. I was tired and awake, satisfied — but able somehow to find touching, teasing and kissing, almost in the most innocent unusual places, reawaken my senses.

"I love you," he whispered.

I could not reply.

* * *

As dawn made its shy appearance, he let go of me for the first time. Then he took me by the hand and we walked together to the window to watch the sun rise before getting ready to complete our journey to Portofino.

We walked past the desk to our awaiting car. The concierge said, "Bon giorno, Signorina Medina."

Holding my head up, I looked him straight in the eye and with great dignity replied, "Bon giorno."

As we got in the car, Guido smiled broadly and said, "I forgot you are an actress."

"So did I for quite a while," replied his leading lady.

Every tree, flower, wave and cloud seemed to be waking up in fresh natural colors to greet the day. The setting was alive for people to fall in love. But, though I was strongly stimulated drinking in the glory of the morning, having shared the passions of the night as never before, I did not love this man. However, I did not want it to be a "one night stand." I had heard that expression and I hated it. It reeked of casual sex. Therefore, it was inevitable that it should last until the end of the picture.

I was experiencing an "affair." The mutual attraction was certainly real and we had given into it. I had had a sad young marriage, but I certainly thought I was in love, or else I would not have married Richard. Then, I had thoroughly enjoyed a "love affair," for in spite of the quarrels and the fear of marriage, there certainly had been love between us.

Now, I was sitting next to a man of whom I needed more, but the one four-letter word that was missing in our relationship was *love*. All these thoughts were hectoring my brain as we faced the enchantment that became Portofino.

We left the car and walked around the harbor. The little ships that sailed slowly in that inviting sea seemed to welcome us. He informed me that he was going to take me directly to the hotel where we were all staying! He was going to check with the crew and the setting, etc. He told me to get some rest as we would be working long hours.

My room naturally overlooked the Mediterranean. As I gazed at it once more, I felt sleepy.

There was a knock at the door. The bellboy handed me a parcel. No card. I opened it. Out fell a nightdress. Oh, but such a rare garment. It was purple chiffon which melded into gold. It was like an Ametrine; a mixture of amethyst and a citrine. I knew he had sent it, but how and where did he find it? The colors were obviously an artist's colors. For one wicked moment, I wondered if he had closets full of them for just such occasions.

I asked him this when I saw him again. His Italian eyes clouded over and I thought that for the first time he might want to hit me. The hurt was so obvious.

The days working were short because they were exteriors and we lost the light. Therefore, the nights were unbelievably long. I accepted and gave every natural sexual urge and marvelously appreciated and needed every final kiss and climax.

He whispered, oh so softly, in my gently caressed ear, "I love you, Patricia."

No reply.

* * *

I finished the picture. I ended the affair. He asked if we could meet again.

I said, "This time the answer is definitely 'no.'" I kissed him and said, *"Addio, e grazie, caro Guido."*

La comedia e finita.

- 8 -

A House is a Home

Back to my home, the Garden of Allah. It was always exciting and interesting for me.

As I was sitting on my terrace one day outside my attractively immoral Errol Flynn bungalow, I saw Leopold Stokowski walk by. He was with two little children. They were his children, though he seemed quite an elderly gentleman at the time. (Gloria Vanderbilt was their mother.) I thought, how wonderful, still great people come here. Then I thought of the greatest people in my life, and I telephoned my mother and father and asked them if they'd like a vacation, to come and stay with me in my new home, The Garden of Allah. They came.

I found a bungalow for them and the first morning, Mummy came dashing into my place. She was quite upset, one might say even angry. They hadn't slept because their bungalow was joined to another and the people next door had come in late and shocked Mummy and Daddy with the noise they were making. I knew the lifeguard from the pool lived there. How foolish of me not to have guessed that he wouldn't spend his nights alone — with that physique and that tan!

I said, "Well, what were they doing, darling? Were they having a party and drinking?"

"No," she said. "Moaning, then oh, yes — moan, moan. It was perfectly shocking — disgusting."

I tried to keep a straight face,. I didn't know what to do. I could visualize that perfect body. With a touch of envy, I realized I had put them next to a virile and highly-sexed man.

"We have to move immediately," said my mother.

My father just looked at me with a slight smile.

"You must go at once to the front desk and tell them we can't stay there."

"Yes, Mummy. I know — but what reason am I going to give? I can't go to the front desk and say, 'You must move my mother and father because the people next door make love all night long.'"

She just tossed that away and said, "Darling, move us please."

My bungalow had another bedroom with a separate entrance so I moved them in there. I had nothing to hide. There were no peculiar noises coming from my place — pity!

We had a very happy month together. I showed them all of California and Daddy was particularly interested in looking at the Pacific and wondering how it all started. He sat gazing and gazing at the sea; his thoughts lost in centuries past. That proud Spanish father of mine was dreaming about his fellow countrymen, their bravery and the excitement that must have filled their beings as they discovered these wondrous foreign shores.

They were such wonderful company. As soon as they left, I was offered a picture in Mexico. It was to be made in Cuernavaca and I was to play opposite Guy Madison. I was to do both versions of the movie: the English and the Spanish.

Off I went to Mexico. I found Mexico City rather like Europe and yet completely different. I like cities — many women do. Mexico City is particularly vigorous, perhaps because of its height which leaves many people breathless. If I was breathless it was because it was exciting: the music, the night life before the movie started. It was all very cosmopolitan.

Before I started the picture, I had to go through the usual medical tests for the company's insurance. A tiny little doctor came into my room. He was very relieved that I spoke Spanish. He said it would make the whole ordeal easier.

He sat down and asked me if I was married. No, I was not. Had I had any heart or lung trouble? No, I had not. Any serious illnesses? No. His final question rather shocked me. He asked me if I was pregnant. No, I was not.

My Spanish was getting very heated and I was quite indignant. I said goodbye to the little fellow and he left.

When I started the picture, I said to the assistant director, Armando Tejas, "I think your doctors are not very tactful."

He said, "What happened?"

"Well, naturally, I had to go through the medical test before we started shooting, and, at first, he asked if I was married, and, of course, I told him that I wasn't. And, after all the other questions, he asked me if I was pregnant! Now, when a young woman arrives in this country and says she isn't married, I do not think they should ask her if she's pregnant."

He agreed and said, "No, I think it's quite wrong to ask her that when she arrives in this country. I think they should ask her when she leaves!"

So much for his attitude, but I don't think it was an attitude. I think it was his sense of humor. And, after all, I suppose I did feed him a straight line. Today, it would have been a straight answer! So?

I loved doing the picture. Guy Madison was easy to work with and a very nice person. When I wasn't working, I would go horseback riding with the stuntmen. I was a little bold, for I am not that great a rider, but galloping in the early morning in Cuernavaca with the wind rushing through my hair was wonderful. It was the most riding I have ever done in my life.

I made another picture in Mexico — that one in the city itself and in Oaxaca. Glenn Ford was the star. The picture was beautiful and was called *Plunder of the Sun*.

Glenn was not easy to work with, not like Alan Ladd and James Mason and Guy. I think he had some personal problem. I learned he had been in love with Rita Hayworth and had never got over her. Well, for that, I can't blame him.

Much later, I was invited for dinner at Glenn's house and as he greeted me he said, "Ah, my favorite leading lady."

Now, I certainly didn't get the feeling that he was being sarcastic, so I guess he's only friendly off the set. Ain't nothing wrong with that I suppose. Yes, there is, it's a rotten attitude.

Picture over. Back to my nest, back to the Garden of Allah. I rested there in my own peculiar feeling of comfort until I was invited to make another picture with Alan Ladd. This time in *England*. What a lovely surprise: *England* and Ladd. I knew them both pretty well.

The production manager at Columbia telephoned me and said, "I suppose you have received the script of the *The Black Knight* that you and Alan are going to make in England."

I informed him happily that I had received it.

a) Mexican actor, Glenn Ford and yours truly.
b) Guy Madison
c) Almost all of me!

"Well, I've just heard from them. They want you to go to Max Factor's and get a blonde wig for yourself and also pick up a slightly darker hairpiece for Alan . . . you know, it's period, so get his a little longer at the back — and take them with you."

"Why? Why do I need a blonde wig? There's nothing in the script that implies I wear one . . . of course, I'll get Alan's 'fall' or whatever it's called —"

"Get your own blonde wig, as well. If you don't use it, it will just come back. They must have had a reason to ask for it."

Off I went to Bob Roberts at Max Factor's. "Find me a gorgeous blonde wig. I've no idea what it's for, but I have to take it to England for Columbia. Also, you have Alan's measurements — I have to take a hairpiece for him. He's playing a knight. You know how they wear their hair."

When Alan and I left for England, they had already shot all the exteriors in Spain. They had to use doubles as neither of us was available for the Spanish shots.

On arriving in England, Lawrence Evans, my agent, telephoned me and I said, "I've brought this glamorous blonde wig. I don't know who'll wear it because there's no reason for me to do a disguise."

He replied, "I don't want to upset you, Patricia, but, when they started shooting in Spain, they didn't have the leading parts cast so they used doubles for all the stunts. A small man played the girl with a full skirt, a bust and a blonde wig. They expect you to play the part as a blonde."

I had a major fit and told Lawrence I had to get to Pinewood Studios to see the producers, Irwin Allen and Cubby Broccoli. I went into the office and I told them exceedingly clearly that I had no intention whatsoever of playing a blonde. I was known as a brunette and that's how I'd play it! Or, they could get Mae West and stick her on a horse and I would return home.

Cubby was very understanding about my outburst. Irwin screamed, called me awful names and said I was *committed*. I replied that I'd have him *committed*, and, hanging onto Lawrence Evans, exited the office, the studio, and, I thought to myself, "after seeing my family, I shall exit the country."

Days went on with discussions between my agent and Irwin Allen. Finally, Irwin said, "There's one scene where Patricia's taken to be burned as a vestal virgin. We could have blonde wigs all over the set and when she's captured, they'd put a blonde wig on her for the scene."

I agreed, thinking it hysterically funny.

The picture went smoothly and happily. When it was over and I saw the rough cut, I thought I looked absolutely ravishing as a blonde vestal virgin. In fact, it was my favorite scene in the picture. I burst into Irwin's office and said, "Why, in the name of Heaven, didn't you ask me to play the picture as a blonde?"

He went crazy. Cubby loved it.

Irwin, I don't think, spoke to me ever again. Cubby's lovely wife, Dana, is a friend of mine to this day and I have been so happy about his well-deserved success with all the Bond pictures.

* * *

In England, I stayed with my family and went to Pinewood Studios every day. On the first day of shooting, the publicity man on the picture, Euan Lloyd (now a very successful independent producer), asked me if I would make an appearance on *What's My Line?* as the mystery guest. Without thinking (as is often my wont), I replied:

"I wouldn't dream of going on that program unless I was one of the panel."

Of course, the four people who were on it had been set for quite some time — and I didn't think giving up a Sunday evening at home to appear for two minutes while I pretended to be someone else was an interesting publicity stunt.

The following day, Euan came to me on the set and said that one of the female panelists had broken her leg, and since I had told him I would happily consider going on the panel, they wanted me for the coming Sunday! I was sick — at myself, at Euan, at the panel and the producer for accepting me, but mainly with myself.

Came the Sunday — naturally, I was in an evening dress, and naturally, I wore one which would compliment me and my figure.

The first contestant went by easily. I believe Gilbert Harding guessed him. The second contestant was a very plain fat woman with a clean and handsome white Scottish terrier.

The questions started. I was now secure. I asked, "Am I right in saying that that poor dog has nothing to do with your work?" (Strong applause from the audience — it was a live show.)

"No," replied the lady.

For those who do not know, or are too young to know (I almost started a song), a "no" means that it passes on to the next person on the four-people panel. Their answers were unsuccessful and the poor contestant could see herself winning about 50 or 100 pounds. (Knowing England, it might have been less.)

Next question, I asked her, "Was your job usually done by a man?

Answer, "No."

The Emcee, Eamonn Andrews, had a little quiet talk with her which I noted. I also noticed that when I asked my second question the audience applauded.

Round again did the questions go until it came back to me. By now I no longer believed her and I was determined that I had not agreed to be on the panel to be made a fool of. So, my next question was loud and clear and fairly confident, "Am I right in saying that this is rather a dirty job?" (Total audience applause.)

Eamonn Andrews spoke quietly to her again. Before he had time to finish, I said, "How is it that every time I ask a question the audience applauds and you say, 'No?' Now, Mr. Andrews, I would like to ask the contestant if she's telling the truth, and I hope the answer is 'no' again."

Eamonn Andrews answered for her. "No," he said quietly.

"Then are you a 'chimney sweep?'" She was indeed and she had to say, "Yes."

But my career was on the line. They only had two channels in England and everybody watched them. I was not a great brain, but I was not a fool, and my appearance this night would reflect on Alan, the picture and me.

The following morning, there was my picture on the front page of the newspaper. In a review (which I wish I had kept, but I have never kept any), Ludovic Kennedy's headline was, "Yes, Miss Medina. You made it."

When I went on the set, dear, gentle Alan said, "Well done."

It meant the world. *What's My Line?* invited me to stay on the panel every Sunday for the duration of the picture. Joan Collins was the mystery guest one Sunday.

While I was still working on the movie, I received a telephone call from Orson Welles. He said he had seen me in a movie and, more recently, he had seen me on *What's My Line?* and he said he had a part for me in a picture that he was making in Spain.

I was so excited to hear from this great director that I said, "Yes, I'd love to do it." I did not hesitate. If he was doing it, I could only learn from him.

- 9 -

The Fortune Teller Genius

I read the script and the moment I finished working with Alan, I flew to Madrid.

In my suite in the hotel, huge bunches of roses arrived welcoming me to Spain, signed Orson Welles. He must have forgotten about the first one for he sent several other arrangements. Then he sent someone round to help me, as I was about to be interviewed by the press.

The P.R. man went back to Orson and said, "She speaks fluent Spanish."

No help needed there. But the wardrobe department called and said I was to buy a nightdress. I was playing (you'll never believe it) a bad girl, and Orson wanted me to get a very sexy nightdress for that scene. I went out looking round the shops in Madrid followed by the wardrobe lady, who was followed by another one. It seems that one was looking after the other. I found it delightful and quite amusing that some places and some people in Spain still were old fashioned enough to protect each other. (It is almost beginning to take over in this country.) You have to be protected. But from bullets!

I walked out with these two chaperons and started looking at nightdresses. By that time I had been in several pictures and obviously, some of them had sneaked into Spain. So the sales-girls would greet me, "Ah, Senorita Medina" and they brought out very innocent, very charming nightdresses.

I said, "No, that wasn't quite right," and we went on, all of them bringing lovely gowns that should only be worn by some moral lady. Finally, I bought one, not at all suited to the part, but I was tired, and embarrassed and I felt very Spanish!

So, I went to the studio followed by the wardrobe lady, followed by the other young lady.

When I went on the set, I saw this great giant. He was heavy but was enormously tall and attractive and brilliant. As he walked toward me and dwarfed me, I said, "Mr. Welles, I don't know if you know it but I'm half Spanish. I did go round those shops but I just couldn't do it. I was afraid they'd think I was either a nursing mother or a prostitute. *So,* I bought one that looks rather like a choir boy's outfit. When they show it to you I would feel terribly relieved if you'd tell them it's perfect. Of course, I won't wear it in the picture. I'll wear one of mine from California."

There was a long pause and the great man looked at me and said, "What kind of a life do you lead in California?"

That was Orson! He thoroughly enjoyed my problem.

As I had not asked Columbia's permission to do this picture, and as I was contracted to start a picture in Hollywood for them in two weeks, I had to tell Orson. I wanted so much to work with him and hoped he could alter the part so I'd play it and return in time to fill my commitment to Columbia.

I was a bit nervous telling him what I had done. He took it noticeably calmly and said, "Well, I suppose we'll just have to kill you off."

Kill me off he did. It made the part shorter but how I remember it! I adored working with Orson. He was, without a doubt, a really great director. His handling of the camera was perfect.

My last scene in the picture before he "killed me off," was a drunk scene I played with him. He was supposed to be one of the richest men in the world, and our scene was to be played on his yacht.

The night before we shot it, I finished work at 11 P.M. Orson called me over to the other set so I could see where I would be working at 6:00 A.M.!

He was shocked when he saw the set. "This looks like a Staten Island Ferry, not a luxury yacht," he muttered disgustedly. "Now, go back to the hotel and get some sleep."

* * *

When I arrived in my room, the telephone was ringing. It was Orson. "Do you have anything in your place that looks as if it would belong on a real yacht?" He continued, "If you find anything, bring it when you come to work."

I said I'd look, and look I did. Through very sleepy eyes I saw a rather nice waste basket with a ship painted on it. "I'll take that," I thought before I went to sleep for a few hours. I tried to forget about "Mr. Arkadin," the film we were making. Orson, of course, played Mr. Arkadin, a multi-millionaire (what else?). I feared the picture would not look very luxurious with that yacht. I laughed as I thought of my elegant contribution — a waste basket!

The following morning I walked on the set. It was unrecognizable. It was glamorous and rich and marvelous.

I discovered that Orson had not been to bed at all. He had been to his hotel and "borrowed" some of the antique furniture from the foyer, had a studio truck and some of the crew sneak in and collect it. Then he arranged the set to his satisfaction.

He saw me staring incredulously. "Patricia, get dressed and we'll play the scene right away. I'd like to get a good shot before they discover it's missing. Then the fellows can return it."

I dressed. We played the scene. He took his time with it and directed me as I have never been directed before. It is my favorite scene of any that I have ever done. Genius is an understatement.

After the movie, he saw me off at the airport because my plane was delayed.

When I arrived in Hollywood, I received a beautiful letter from Orson complimenting me on my comedy.

Then another short note from the production manager asking me to please send them a glamour still, as they needed it to have it blown up so that they could use it in the picture, and also in advertising it.

To my shame, I never answered Orson's letter. I treasured it, but I didn't answer it. Also, I forgot all about the still picture the production wanted.

I rushed straight to work for Columbia. I was extremely tired as I had to work with Orson until midnight every night so I could get back to California in time not to break my contract.

Also, I fainted once on the set at Columbia, and then, as they had found out I had made the picture in Spain, they gave it to the press that I had been overworked, as they had no union hours in Spain. They blamed my tiredness on Mr. Welles!

I had to go to Paris to dub Orson's picture. I sat in the projection room waiting for him, longing to see this director that I admired so much. He finally came in and said, "Good morning." And that was all!

I was very disappointed and guessed that my ill manners had caused this. "Orson, I'm so very sorry I didn't answer your letter. I have kept it; I was so thrilled to receive it. I had to work non-stop from the moment I got there, remember I was late at Columbia."

He nodded his head. "You didn't send me the photograph I needed for the picture."

I said, "No. I'm so sorry."

"We had to concoct a picture our of two of yours we found."

He showed me the one they had made up. "Oh what a horrible picture, what are my arms doing up in the air like that?"

"Just be thankful I did not put hair under your arms, as I'm not feeling very friendly towards you, Miss Medina."

I was upset. "Orson, don't be silly. Take me to lunch and let's be friendly like we were on the picture."

Rather grudgingly he did take me out to lunch and during lunch he said, "You know you're really very difficult."

I decided that I had apologized enough so I said, "I thought you recognized difficulty."

He said, "Yes, I do, and in some ways I like it very much. It shows character, but you're really too much for me to cope with. The only person who could handle you would be my best friend."

I said inquiringly, "Well, who is your best friend?"

"Joseph Cotten," he replied.

"Oh, I've met Jo Cotten and his wife many times at David and Jennifer Selznick's. She's a darling and has a wonderful sense of humor, and he's certainly very attractive and quite one of the best actors I've ever seen. Oops, have I offended you again?"

He smiled and said, "No, I happen to agree with you."

"Oh, agreement at last. I'll drink to that." I was relieved. "Anyway, I don't know them very well," I said.

"That doesn't matter."

He ordered the wine that I thought would cement our friendship. But after the fish and the dessert, I knew that for this meeting, at least, he was going to nurture his hurt.

Apparently, he couldn't quite cope with me. I didn't really believe it. I just think he was offended at my unexpected bad manners, and I did not think he had written many fan letters.

He taught me on and off the picture! I had a feeling we'd meet again and everything would be all right.

- 10 -

Bette the Great

So, I returned to California and my nest.

I was going to do a television film for a very good friend of mine, William Frye. He is still one of my best friends in the world.

When I went on the set to see him, he had just finished a film with Bette Davis, and he introduced me to the great actress. She was very polite and charming, and she told me that she was going to give an award at the Academy Awards ceremony in a couple of weeks' time, and she asked me if I'd like to go with Bill Frye. I said I'd love it. We were to have dinner at her home first.

It took me a long time to choose a dress for this great occasion. The Academy Awards. I had never seen them *and* I was going to dinner with one of the finest actors of all time. So I selected an off-the-shoulder, scarlet chiffon dress, after all, I was not going to let her down, and I wore a silver blue mink coat which was my pride and joy.

The evening came and Bill picked me up and we arrived at Bette's house. *She* was standing behind the bar in a bottle green dress (not a very nice dress), and it was during her plump period. So there she was, shaking a martini and looking rather like an unmade bed.

I said, "good evening," walked across the room and as I flung my coat carelessly on the sofa, she said, in that unmistakable voice of hers, "Pat, how kind of you to dress so inconspicuously."

I loved that remark. She never let me down. Aside from her monumental talent, she was a very complicated and interesting woman. If she liked you, you were rare and honored. If she didn't, God help you.

Before we left for the ceremony, Bette managed to make herself look pretty — although, I wish I'd known her well enough to ask her to change the green velvet dress. Actually, I'm very glad that I did not, for it occurred to me later that probably no one knew Bette Davis well enough to ask her to change her mind about anything!

There were crowds of fans outside the auditorium and they flocked adoringly after Bette, pleading for her royal signature. The police kept most of them under control. Those that managed to get close enough, clutching their pictures and their pens, were rewarded with an icy smile and a regal flourish of her green velvet "tea cozy" as she floated in. It was a performance worthy of her fourth award . . . or was it her fifth?!

We walked at a respectable distance behind her. It was difficult for me to appear so sophisticated. All I wanted to do was gaze at the movie stars, at their glittering clothes and see who was with whom — I had been so bored and laid-back during all the time I had been in Los Angeles, having only seen administration buildings, studios, make-up rooms, wardrobe departments, etc. When I wasn't working on some insignificant picture, I was sitting home waiting for stardom to come my way.

This was what I had expected. This was Hollywood! I had pictured myself as a star looking glamorous and successful with cameras photographing me from all angles. I knew I could act. After all, Louis B. Mayer said he sensed stardom. He had signed me for three straight years — then he disappeared before he could fulfill his promise. I was left doing nothing and nobody knew I was under contract! Harry Cohn had "sensed stardom" but M.G.M. wouldn't release me — then, when I was free, Mr. Cohn died. Had I come six thousand miles from home to kill off the heads of studios? It never occurred to me that I should have helped myself and worked at becoming known like most of these famous actresses that I was resenting and envying. I pulled myself together and let the tears that were about to fall just brighten my eyes as I followed Bette like a bridesmaid in my beautiful red chiffon dress. I was not envious of Bette, and I admired her enormously.

Occasionally, I looked at some of the other people. They smiled at me. Most of them were stars and they deserved to be. I forgot my envy and smiled back at them, proud to be in their company.

When we arrived at our seats, Bette said, "I'll sit with you for a while, then I'll have to go backstage and get ready for my appearance *giving* that wretched award." She said this rather loudly and, although a few people looked at her disapprovingly, it did not faze her one iota. She took her seat with a "thud" and then closed her eyes as if the whole thing would not be worth watching until her entrance.

I smiled with affection and understanding at her autocratic attitude. She was about the most important person there and I couldn't think why she'd agreed to *give* an award.

Quite soon, she left her seat and went backstage. I cannot remember who appeared on the show. Who won that award? I was wondering what Bette would say, how she would look and who she would give the award to. There was much applause and I leaned forward expecting her to appear on stage and in her inimitable voice make her announcement.

Instead, to my amazement and momentary horror, she appeared in the aisle at the end of our row and said, "Come along, we're leaving."

Bill and I got up, stunned and apprehensive. She walked ahead and said not a word until we were in the limousine. Then she let go!

"Some of those amateurs receiving awards talked much too long. So, if I had given my award, they wouldn't have had time for the Best Actor or the Best Picture. Hah!," she said in a low, full voice. "They're all amateurs. They didn't know how to put on a show. They'll have to limit the time that people spend thanking two hundred and fifty friends. Next they'll be thanking their dogs — hah," she said again. "That's the last thing I'll do for them. I need a drink."

We all did.

The moment we arrived at Bette's, Bill rushed into the house and got the drinks from the bar.

"It was a dreadful show," said Bill, most convincingly.

"They ought to have got you to produce it," said our hostess.

We agreed that Bill would have done much better.

Bette finished her drink in a trice and went behind the bar and poured herself another large one. "Gary should be here soon," she announced out of the blue.

"You'll be pleased to see him, I'm sure," said I, hoping he would come walking in any minute and make her forget the show and we could finish the evening happily.

"Sure, I'll be glad to see the s.o.b., and, as soon as he gets here, you can all vanish."

"Where's he coming from?" as I went to get my coat.

"San Francisco."

"That's not very far. He should be here any minute," I continued. The evening had ended long ago as far as I was concerned.

Bette went to the front door, gazed out expectantly and then returned to refill her glass.

Finally, I dared to speak my thoughts. "If you want to see him looking desirable, I wouldn't have another drink."

She glared at me and then laughed. "Oh my God, child, you're romantic. He's probably walking home. If he's not here by now, he'll probably crawl up the drive on all fours. Let's face it, there's no reason this evening should have a happy ending. Goodnight, all."

I already had my coat. Bill grabbed my hand and we flew the coop before she could change her mind.

* * *

Some weeks later, I was at a big party at Janet Gaynor and her husband Adrian's home (Adrian was the famous dress designer and he was not well at the time). It was a beautiful house in perfect taste. Bette and Gary Merrill were there. Bette had a black dress on and looked very nice. I had not seen her since the *non*-award evening — but I did write her a note thanking her for the dinner. I also wrote that I was glad she hadn't given the award that evening because I said it would not have seemed right to see Bette Davis *giving* an award instead of *receiving* one. She had given enough to the Academy with all her magnificent performances — she did not have to demean herself by coming on stage from the back. People only wanted to see her walk from the audience up the steps and be met by a fine actor who would hand her one of the many statues she deserved.

At the Adrian's party, she greeted me very warmly, then she said, "Pa*tt* (she always hit the t's so hard it sounded as if I had two), I would like you to do something for me."

"Of course, Bette. What is it?"

"I would like you to educate Gary, then give him back to me."

"There's only one problem," I replied.

"What's that?"

"If I educate him, he might not want to come back."

We looked into each other's eyes for what seemed an eternity. Then she flung her arms round me and said, "You are the most honest, intelligent and humorous person out here."

At that moment, Gary came over. He had a drink in his hand. "Hello, you two," he said.

"Gary, I want you to meet my friend Patricia Medina," said Bette.

He shook my hand and gave me an ingratiating smile.

* * *

I went to Bette's house several times to small and large parties. Gary was never there. They were certainly separated — I do not think divorced, yet. She never discussed it with me and I never asked anyone about it. Bette was an excellent cook and she entertained beautifully. Apparently, they *were* divorced — I never knew when; perhaps, earlier than I thought, for Bette never seemed quite her vital, vibrant self.

However, one day my telephone rang and a voice said, "Miss Medina, this is Gary Merrill. We met when I was married to Bette Davis."

"Yes," I said, "I remember. . ."

"I was wondering if you would have dinner with me one evening."

"Oh, Mr. Merrill. I'm sorry, I cannot."

"Well, it doesn't have to be immediate. I could call you next week?"

"I must ask you not to call me anymore as I will not be having dinner with you. It's nothing against you, personally, but Bette is a friend of mine."

It was swell while it lasted, but then Bette and Gary had a "bumpy ride."

"Miss Medina, she and I have been divorced for quite some time. There would be nothing wrong in our having dinner together. I think I would know how to behave, and you said you had nothing against me personally."

"However long you and Bette have been divorced has nothing to do with my refusal. This may sound odd to you, but I just do not go out with my friends' ex-husbands. Therefore, it would be a waste of time for you to telephone me again. Is that clear?"

"Yes, very. Goodbye."

"Goodbye."

I never told anyone about that telephone conversation. It was no one's business. *But* sometime later, mutual friends of Bette's and mine said she had told them the story and she thought I was a rare friend. Who told her? It had to be Gary confessing to his ex-wife because it certainly didn't come from me.

* * *

My father became quite sick, so I took a rather hurried trip to England to be with him. We discovered it wasn't serious and I was able to stay until he got better. We had many talks together and once he said:

"It's so nice to have you here with us at home, darling. Are you going to come back?"

I said, "I'll always come back to see you and Mummy, and Piti and Gloria, but, you know I live in the United States."

He said, "Yes, darling, I know, but who's looking after you?"

"Well," I said, "I have a lot of friends and I don't really need anyone to look after me."

"I worry about you. I'm getting older. You see, Piti has Ken and Gloria has Gerry, and I don't worry about them, but I do worry about you. I wish you were married."

And I had to say, "Daddy, I love you very much. I don't want you to worry, but you see marriage just isn't for me. I am looked after. I'll come and see you all and you will come and see me, but marriage — *no.*"

He looked at me rather sadly and shook his head. We kissed each other until the next time.

* * *

When I arrived back home to California, I read in the paper that Rex Harrison's wife, actress Kay Kendall, had died of leukemia. I knew them very well and I was deeply sorry for Rex. Kay had been a real fun person.

I was thinking about the really crazy time we had in England. It seemed totally impossible that Kay's laughter had stopped. It was a necessary sound, and, as I thought of her, I heard her.

One of the wildest times I will always remember was when Simone Signoret, Kay and I had lunch at The Caprice in London. Simone had not long before finished giving a superb performance in *Room at The Top*. She invited Kay and me to lunch to celebrate her great reviews. We had a magnum of champagne and Kay started by saying, "We'll have two glasses each right away, and, then in turns, we'll tell our funniest experience. No holding back — truthful, funny memories. OK?"

We said, "Okay," with bubbles in our throats.

Simone started. I can't remember her story but she was hysterical. Being such a magnificent actress, I'm sure she exaggerated, but it didn't matter. Kay and I were screaming with laughter.

The guests at tables around us ceased to talk and listened to our conversation and they started to laugh. By the time it got to my turn, the whole restaurant was laughing and gentlemen were sending us more champagne along with flowers. We accepted them as an audience. We accepted their gifts.

"Sexy Rexy." He and Jo were my "bookends" when I was on crutches. Marvelous actor, good friend—but boy did he live up to his nickname!

All of a sudden it became the talk of London; people walked in, who didn't have tables, and joined in the party.

Finally, Jimmy Woolf, who, with his older brother John, had produced *Room at The Top,* came in and said, "I'm in charge of these terrible ladies and I'm taking them each home in a limousine because they're having dinner with me tonight and I think they should have a rest first."

Simone was not given a check. Jimmy rushed us out, tears of laughter running down our cheeks and the whole restaurant applauded either because of our stories or because we were leaving!

I had known Kay well, and her wild sense of fun did not surprise me. Simone did. I was such a fan of hers that when I got to know her, I was not prepared for her "off stage" persona. She was a woman prepared to enjoy every moment to the fullest when she wasn't working. Her laughter was loud and her humor on the boisterous side. Kay was feminine. Simone was womanly.

* * *

My thoughts then floated to Lenore Cotten. She was a really good friend of mine; she also had a great sense of humor. About the same time that Rex was experiencing his tragedy, Jo Cotten had lost his wife Lenore, also to leukemia.

Now the laughter had stopped. These two unhappy, good friends would be coming back to California — Rex, to do a film; Jo, to pick up his life, such as it was, and to make more pictures, I presumed.

I had lost two very good friends and I knew I would miss them greatly. Two lone husbands were returning to their careers and their empty houses.

* * *

I went to David and Jennifer's house and had such a lovely evening there. There was the usual group of friends: Billy Wilder, that great director, and his wife Audrey, Sammy Goldwyn and Peggy, and Leonard Gersch. Even Truman Capote crept in. It was a happy group of fun people. David Niven and Hjordis, who was a close friend of mine, were there also.

I spent a lot of time at the Niven's. We called their house the "Pink House" — because it was painted pink — now, wasn't that original? It took us a long time to think up that name!

* * *

I have never had a brother but the nearest person I knew who could have been my brother was David Niven. I knew him slightly in England much earlier when I was just starting in pictures. Niv had returned to England to fight for his country in World War II, leaving a flourishing career in Hollywood for the honor of joining the British Army. He was the first Englishman to leave Hollywood during the war. Others followed his patriotic lead.

David was released for three months from the Army to make a movie. They needed a star occasionally to do their film work and cheer up their fellow countrymen.

In David's picture there was one line to be said to him by an Italian girl. As I had absolutely no experience whatsoever, but I did look Italian, I was asked to jump out of a gondola with a bunch of flowers which I was to give to Niv and say the immortal words, "These are for you" —

David Niven. Niv and I could have been brother and sistser. His wife was a close friend of mine. He was a great wit, a fine actor, and a wonderful friend.

Take One. I jumped out of the gondola, tripped, and, as I landed, I dropped the flowers. Undeterred, I ran to Niven and said in my perfect Italian accent, "Those were for you." David burst out laughing, the director screamed "*Cut*" and we did it again.

Take Two. This time, I didn't trip but ran gracefully to David and was starting my line. (It was a close shot on me, over David's shoulder.) He crossed his eyes and I burst out laughing!

Take Three. Unknown actress with one line: As I reached David the third time, we looked into each others eyes and both of us broke-up laughing with tears streaming down our cheeks, trying to control ourselves. We were told to sit down, get serious and concentrate on the movie.

"How do we do that?" said the budding star to the experienced actor. He turned away from me to laugh and we became brother and sister.

After the tenth take, they printed it and I was sent home. We didn't meet again until I was in Hollywood, married to Richard. I became very good friends with David's wife, Hjordis, a beautiful Swedish girl. We were a sort of crazy family when I was divorced.

David announced one day that the picture was coming on television that evening. He told his sons, David Jr. and Jamie, and Hjordis, that we were all to sit and watch my big film debut with him as the little Italian girl. We were both quite indignant to discover that our famous scene had been eliminated!

Once, when Hjordis was in the hospital, having a minor operation, I went to see her every day. We talked and laughed, which hurt the stitches in her tummy.

"Don't talk, Pat," she said. "I don't want to laugh anymore."

Niven came in on cue, kissed his wife and said, "Aren't you lucky to have us both here to make you well."

I got up on cue and said, "I'll leave you two. I have to go home and wash my hair."

Niv said, "Stay a while. We're right near the ocean. Let's go and have a drink and a sandwich. The cook's off tonight and I have to eat."

"And I have to wash my hair."

Hjordis added, "Oh Pat, go and have a bite with poor David. You can wash your hair later."

"It won't look any better clean," said my kindly *brother.*

Hjordis was tired and got rid of us both.

I left my car at St. John's Hospital and jumped in with Niv. "Don't go too far — I really do have to go home and wash my hair."

He stopped the car right away in the middle of street: "Is this far enough?"

"Don't be a damn fool. I'm hungry."

We drove on in silence. Along the Coast Highway, we saw a pretty place on the ocean with a garden in front.

"Want to try this?"

"Why not."

In we walked. It was attractive and had little cubicles overlooking the Pacific Ocean.

The waiter came. "We'll have a glass of white wine each and a menu, please," said Niv.

The waiter walked off and pulled a curtain round us. Of all the couples in Hollywood who would not find this a romantic enclosure, Niv and I were the two.

"Open this curtain," I said loudly.

The waiter responded, "That's the way we serve here — so you can enjoy the privacy and the ocean." He was gone.

Niv got up to pull the curtain open; it wouldn't move. "If you laugh, Pat, I'll kill you," he said in hysterics of laughter. We were kidnapped.

"I have to go home and wash my hair."

"Oh, shut up!"

"Why?"

"Because this isn't just a restaurant."

"What is it?"

"I think it's a whore house."

I gave a scream of laughter and accidently broke my chair. We laughed so much —

The waiter returned, opened the curtains with two drinks on a little tray. "Please be quiet. What do you want?"

"My check," said Niv, holding the curtain. "Or else I'll. . ."

"Here is your check. Please go," said the waiter.

I ran out to the car and jumped in. Niv arrived looking stunned.

"What now?" I said, trying not to laugh.

"I think I paid for a room," said Niv.

We drove back to the hospital where I'd left my car. We wanted to tell Hjordis but it was too late.

"Well, goodnight and thanks for nothing," I said.

"Oh, go home and wash that God awful hair of yours."

"How much was my half of the room?"

"It was a double bed."

"How do you know?"

He stopped the car and we finally gave in to hysterical laughter. "I wish Hjordis was awake. We'd have to wait till tomorrow to tell her what happens to us when she gets sick," I said.

I got out of the car. "I'm too weak now to wash my hair."

As I ran to my car, Niv followed to open my door. "I'm sorry, darling," he said.

A nun passed by and said, "Quiet. This is a hospital."

"I apologize, Sister," he said.

"Oh, that's alright," I said.

David vanished in a flash!

Of course, we told Hjordis —

Some weeks later, she and I were having lunch in their garden. "Where's that place that you and David went to when I was ill?" Hjordis inquired.

"Why?"

"I want to give a little surprise lunch for David's birthday on Sunday — just Larry Olivier, Peter Ustinov and Susanne, and the three of us."

"David will never do it," I replied.

"I have a plan. First, do you think you could find it?"

"I'll try. Want to go now?"

We got in my car. After two mistakes, I found it because of the garden. We booked a table in the dining room on Sunday. Mission accomplished, we went home to make a plan.

On Sunday, I went in the morning early and wished Niv a happy birthday. However, he pleaded that I stay and have lunch and he'd ask Larry. I said I simply had to read a script and he and Hjordis should have a quiet happy day together.

"Don't call Larry," I said, hoping he'd obey me.

I got away and went to the house Larry was renting. Peter Ustinov (a highly successful playwright and actor, and also the funniest man I know) and his then wife, Susanne, were there waiting for me.

Now, it was up to Hjordis to get Niv to the beach, but, harder still to get him into our *house*. I had faith in her. He usually gave in if she asked. This time, she'd have to beg — and *did*.

She managed to get him to the beach without much trouble, but when she said, "Just take me to that place you and Pat went to," he said, "*no*." She said she just wanted to look in the entrance — not sit down.

Meantime, we four got into Larry's open car and drove along the Coast Highway. Peter and Susanne were in the back. Peter at that time was wearing a full, dark, fairly long beard. I was in the front with Larry.

I was getting nervous in case we spotted the Niven's car — actually, more nervous that they would see us. "Can you put the top up? Peter is very conspicuous back there."

Larry put the top up.

Peter said, "Thank you. I've been rather afraid of being shot!"

We arrived at our destination and went into the dining room, which we booked only for our group.

A little later, the Nivens walked in the hallway. Larry was talking to me quietly and I laughed. Niv recognized the laugh — turned round and saw Larry and me. He said quietly

to Hjordis, "Quick, let's get out of here. Pat and Larry are here . . . they'd be so embarrassed if we saw them."

Hjordis laughed, we all laughed and pulled Niven in and wished him a happy birthday! And it was . . .

* * *

People would "drop in" at the Niven's: Larry Olivier, Peter Ustinov, Noel Coward and many others from the old country.

Oh, yes, a few Americans were there quite often. For instance, we often had dinner quietly in the den. Just David and Hjordis, Fred Astaire and yours truly.

Larry Olivier, the greatest actor in England. Director, producer, friend. His life was the stage.

Fred was quiet, gentle and very easy to get along with.

One night the Niv's were having a very weighty conversation that didn't concern either of us — so, Fred said to me, "Let's go to the other room and turn on some music."

Off we trotted to the living room and Fred turned on the music.

He came and put his arm round me as if to dance. I say "as if" because it was the most disastrous caricature of two people attempting to ballroom dance. The fact that one of them was Fred Astaire made it more pathetic.

He pulled me toward him and took one step back. I promptly put my foot on top of *his* multimillion dollar foot. He reacted by treading on my other foot. I either had to laugh or cry.

Deciding to do the former, I pushed him away and said, "Fred, wherever did you get the idea that you could dance?"

Ignoring my stupid remark, he let go of me and took a flying leap onto a round table in the center of the room. He danced on that table for about ten minutes. It was sheer beauty.

When we returned to the den, David said, "Where have you two been?"

"Oh, we just went in the other room to have a little dance," said the gentleman.

One evening, Fred invited the three of us to The Beachcombers in Hollywood. It was a pleasant, very amicable evening.

We went back to the "Pink House" and I took off in my independent motor car for my nest.

The next day, Hedda Hopper had in her column, "The best kept secret in town is the romance blooming between Patricia Medina and Fred Astaire."

Well, it was indeed a very well kept secret, for neither Fred nor I knew about it.

We did not go out to restaurants again. Just ate in the den. Neither of us needed the gossip. Fred was having a romance with his dancing partner, Barrie Chase — a superb dancer. And I had avoided being involved romantically with anyone.

The closest I'd ever got to Fred was when I trod on his toes!

Some nights later, they gave a small party and Niven introduced me to Cole Porter. He was a sophisticated gentleman with such style. He sported a red carnation and leaned heavily on an elegant walking stick. He had a severe injury when he was very young which was never cured and he suffered great pain.

For some reason, he took a liking to me. We hit it off from the moment we met. I found him enchanting. His command of the English language was magically unique. Of course, he manifested that in most of the lyrics of his many famous songs. He found me amusing and quick witted. With him, what else could one be?

A few days later, he invited me to his home for dinner. I was rather nervous. I knew it would be a chic gathering. I also discovered that if one was invited for 7:00 P.M. in Hollywood you were expected to arrive considerably later. Since I was alone, I chose my dress carefully and waited a while before leaving as I did not want to be the first to arrive. The telephone rang.

It was Niv calling me from Cole's study where no one could hear him. "Where the hell are you. He's giving this dinner in your honor and he's getting very angry. I think he might just go into dinner early to teach you a lesson. For God's sake get with it." He hung up.

I jumped into my dress, dashed into the car, combing my hair on the way and driving like a mad thing along Sunset Boulevard to his street (which I had never been to).

The butler opened the door and said, "They are all at dinner. I'll take you in."

Putting my shoulders back, I followed him through the living room and into the dining room.

"Miss Medina," he announced in rather scathing tones.

I beheld an enormous round table with about eleven people seated. Cole leaned back in his chair and stared questionably at me. He couldn't stand up without being helped and even if he could have, I felt that he wouldn't. He definitely had had dinner earlier than planned.

I looked directly at him and said, "Oh Cole, I do apologize for being late, but I had no idea you were so suburban!"

I then went and took my place next to Niv and took a large gulp of wine before I dared look Cole's way again. He was smiling!

I was a little late. He did not tell me the party was in my honor. Had I known, I would have been there on time or a little early. He was a devil. He wanted me to grovel but liked me very much for throwing the ball into his court.

After dinner, he was charming. He made me feel like a friend and he was indeed a friend, for the rest of his life. What an interesting, brilliant, complicated man.

As I was driving home along Sunset, a car pulled up beside me and honked. I took a quick look — it was Clark. He went on honking until we got to a red light, then we opened our windows.

"Are you gong to marry Fred Astaire?" he boomed.

"No. Are you going to marry Silvia Ashley?"

He muttered a four-letter word and drove off in a rush.

He did marry Silvia Ashley. It was the worst mistake they both made.

I saw them together — well, together and apart — at a big party at Bill Goetz's house. She had had too much to drink and he looked cold and angry, *sans* that wondrous twinkle that I remembered.

I got up to leave and he followed me. He walked me to my car and opened the door. I was about to get in when he turned me and kissed me fully on the lips. I did not push him away. I felt he deserved an ending to something that had never come to fruition — and never would.

Still holding me, he said, "I suppose you've heard that I'm the worst lay in town."

"That makes two of us," I said lightly as I got into the car. "You shouldn't have married a limey."

"Sure picked the wrong one," he slammed the car door on his reply.

I liked him. Even angry, he was manly, not petty.

I saw him once before he died. He was with Kay, his last wife, and he certainly hit the jackpot with her.

He was sitting beside me on a sofa and we were laughing. Suddenly, Kay said, "Cool it, Pa, and come over here."

He gave me a wicked grin, got up and went and sat beside his lovely wife.

I was really happy when he married Kay. They had one son, whom he never met. *The King* did not live long enough.

* * *

Lying in bed one cold Sunday morning, I pulled up the covers over my red flannel night dress and prepared to sleep a little longer, when I heard a loud noise and voices at my living room window, and the window being forced open.

I sat bolt upright, scared stiff, when staggering into my bedroom, the fumes of alcohol preceding them, came Robert Coote and Collier Young. Coote (as we all called him) was a really good comic actor and a close friend of Niv's. Collier was a writer/producer and a wit. He had married Ida Lupino and they'd had a production company. She directed and acted; he produced and wrote.

Well, here they were roaring drunk *in my bedroom* with their arms around each other. Since I was speechless, Coote started: "Listen, Medina," he said. "My friend Collie and I have decided that it's high time you got married."

He paused to lean on the furniture, so Collier decided he'd better continue: "We've made a deal, you have to choose between Cootie and me."

Cootie picked up the slack, "If you choose Collie-boy, then I'll bow out."

Collier said, "If you choose Cootie, I will bow out." He made an attempt at bowing.

Finally, I found my voice. "Will you both bow out of here at once . . ."

Before I could continue, Coote interrupted me, "It's your last chance, Medina. You're not getting any younger and you'll never get a chance like this again. Now which one of us do you want?"

I couldn't contain my laughter. I tried very seriously to ask them to leave. They were holding each other up and I was afraid they'd fall — then what would I do?

"Listen, you poor excuses for gentlemen. Go as quietly as you can and leave the way you came in. I'll shut the window after you. Go and have some coffee and don't come back to see me until you are clean and sober and preferably married. And knock at the door."

I became very dignified in my red flannel nightdress. "I am the only person (I think) with a reputation, a fairly good reputation in this historical, hysterical remnants of a hotel or apartment house. Whatever. Now leave."

The need for another drink, or the fact that I was boring them sick, made them decide to leave.

But Cootie wouldn't go quietly. "You'll regret this all your life, won't she, chum?" he said to Collie who looked as if he hadn't heard him.

There was an awful noise of giggles and stumbles. When I thought the coast was clear, I went and locked the living room window and returned to my bed.

They were really nice people, both of them. *But* they had tied one on perhaps at the bar at the Garden of Allah, and there got the great idea of breaking and entering and (as they thought) amusing an old friend.

It occurred to me that Collier should have lived at the Garden of Allah at the time of Fitzgerald and Benchley. He had the wit and the ability to keep up with them and their liquor consumption. However, he was not of that era. He succeeded sometime later, and obviously while sober, in marrying Joan Fontaine, a fine and beautiful actress. I don't believe it lasted very long, her career being more successful than his.

Having lost out with two good actresses, he finally married a girl not in the business. Meg had a shop that sold babies' clothes. They married, she moved into his house and they were perfectly happy (as far as I know).

Coote was cut out to be a bachelor. Although he had a crush on all his friends' wives, he never married. He was a dear friend, and he saved many women a life of hell by staying single.

I spent all Sunday in bed, got up in the afternoon, and had some tea and toast and settled down to read and rest in my permanent Flynn bungalow.

* * *

The following morning, I heard some very distressing rumors, at least I hoped they were rumors. The "Garden of Allah" was going to be razed. This was an awful shock. A great personal shock. To lose such a special place was dreadful.

Then, I suddenly had a great idea. I thought they were going to knock down all the bungalows, shouldn't I buy my bungalow and move it somewhere. So I called the office and asked who was going to do this destruction, and they told me the name of the company: The Cleveland Wrecking Company.

I called The Cleveland Wrecking Company and said I would like to talk to them if someone would come round and see me. I set the appointment for the following afternoon.

I had just had a shower and washed my hair, when I heard a loud knock at the front door. I grabbed some slacks and a shirt, didn't have time to put a comb through my wet, straggly hair, and I opened the door. There stood Adonis himself — the most handsome man I have ever seen was apologizing to me for arriving early. He was charming and didn't seem upset by my soaking wet hair, and my non-made-up face. He told me he was from The Cleveland Wrecking Company, looked around and said, "What a lovely bungalow."

"That's how I feel," I said sincerely (I looked so ghastly, I had to be sincere). "Since you are going to . . . raze all these buildings, is there any way that I could buy this bungalow and move it to some lot, and how much would it cost?"

He said, "Well, it would cost you what it would take us to destroy it." He looked at the windows and all the doors, etc. and figured that it would come to a few thousand dollars.

"Where do you want to move it?"

I said, "I really don't know," and he gave me a terribly strong look as if to say — "Oh, the poor thing is insane."

I said, "When are you going to demolish it? Give me a week and I'll find somewhere."

He said, "Well, it will be just about a week, and we'll be in touch again."

* * *

I had to have advice from someone who understood my particular idiosyncrasies.

There was only one person to call: Ruthie Esmond. (After all, she'd risked her life in my motor car.) I hold her responsible for my writing these pages. She encouraged, cajoled, criticized and nagged me to write and continue writing. I'm still not sure whether to thank her or to blame her! Anyway, I had to talk to her about my house problem.

"Ruthie," I said, "I want to move my bungalow somewhere."

She said, "I see." Pause. It did not surprise her at all that I wanted to move a building round the town.

"Do you know where I could put it?"

"You could put it in the street outside our house," she said, obviously manifesting that we had our insanity in common.

I said I didn't think they'd allow me to do that. So, she found a few pieces of land near them that were already sold.

Thanks a lot, friend!

The next day I thought it would be lovely to have that bungalow sitting on the beach.

I found a lot near Malibu that would be perfect for not a frightening price at all. Today, it's ludicrous. It was something like fifteen thousand dollars.

I called The Cleveland Wrecking Company where I thought I could make a deal and buy it. They said, "We couldn't possibly get this building under the bridge where you want to go." They checked and said, "No, it wouldn't work."

That was the end of my Malibu thing.

Well, to make a long story short, my week was up and I didn't get my bungalow. I had told the people at the office. They knew my idea and liked it, but since I hadn't acquired a lot, I certainly couldn't move it, and they said, "I'm sorry, but we're going to have to ask you to leave."

Somebody wrote that I was the last celebrity to live in the Garden of Allah. I really don't think I was much of a celebrity, though, at that time, I was as close as I ever would be, I suppose.

Well, I made several trips carrying my clothes in my arms, with tears streaming down my face, out of the Garden of Allah and across the street into the Chateau Marmont, a large building that was constantly frequented by actors and authors from all over the world. Whenever they came to work in Hollywood, that was their chosen home.

I was on the top floor at the Chateau Marmont. I had a balcony and I would look out toward all the buildings that had gone at the "Garden of Allah." My bungalow remained, and I have often wondered if it was because of my idea that I'd passed on to one of the owners. *He* had found a convenient lot nearby to move it. I don't know this to be true, but I did wonder.

There is no "Garden of Allah" anymore. I think there's a bank building there. There is a little glass case with a miniature of that historic building. Somehow, someone felt that a replica should be kept.

- 11 -

Yes! Yes! Yes!

Not long after I had moved into the Chateau Marmont, I received a letter from Richard. He was on his yacht, somewhere in the Mediterranean. He told me that he had asked someone to marry him. He said that she was half English and half Spanish and he thought that might have attracted him. However, he said he regretted very much having asked her and that if I would meet him anywhere in the world, anywhere I suggested, he would fly over and we could maybe try again. Poor Richard. He never gave up trying.

I sat down and I wrote him, I hoped, an understanding letter. I told him that he was possibly oversentimentalizing our years together and apart, and that I was sure that if he had asked someone to marry him, she must be very nice. I said, please make a life for yourself if you're lonely, and I think you are. And I wished him all the happiness in the world.

He did marry the lady in question and they were not really very happy. I always thought he should have married the girl he met on Capri years ago. All that has gone by the board now and so has poor Richard since then. He was far too young to die. He contracted pneumonia after his accident and never recovered.

I was fairly happy at the Chateau. They were awfully nice people. And I worked from there, and I partied from there, and I used my motor car.

Then I went on Saturdays to visit Rexy and cheer him up, and, together with the Nivens, I went to visit Jo Cotten every Sunday. Sally Foster was there, and a lot of ladies — mostly ladies to cheer him up.

Every Sunday we went for over a month. And then the Nivens went to New York and Jo said, "I hope this doesn't mean that you're not going to come and see me."

I said, "Oh, no. Of course, I'll come and Sally will come and Jennifer will come. The Nivens are going on to England or Switzerland, so they'll be away for a long time. So don't worry, we'll all come and see you. Rexy on Saturday, and you on Sunday." I think he was very glad to hear it.

One night, Jennifer Jones called and said, "Don't you think it's time Rexy and Jo get out of their houses. Why don't you bring them both up to dinner here? Jo can pick up Rex and then together they can pick you up."

I thought this was a fine idea, since I'd broken my ankle and I had crutches.

I called them both and asked them if they would be my "book ends." With that agreed by all, Rexy and Jo and I would go up every week to have dinner with Jennifer Jones and David

Beautiful Jennifer Jones. Academy award winner and very dear friend with husband, David O. Selznick, producer of Gone with the Wind *and many other pictures.*

Selznick in their lovely house. They were very generous people and my two "bookends" were both gallant.

But one of them suddenly announced that he had to go away. Jo Cotten had been offered a picture in Mexico. He was to go away for three months.

The next time that Jennifer gave a dinner party, I telephoned her. "Jennie," I said. "let me come by myself. Don't ask Rexy to bring me, I'd really rather not."

She said, "Oh, fine. All right." And then, "By the way, Pat, if it were Jo who was going to bring you on his own, what would you say??" She laughed and hung up the telephone. Jennifer is a very wise woman.

So on my own, I went up to the Selznick's. As usual, it was bright and lively and friendly. I hadn't realized how dependent I had become on them.

David came up to me and said, "I've been talking to Jo Cotten. He's awfully lonely. Why don't you go down there. You speak Spanish. You could have fun there."

I said, "David, I'm not going to Mexico."

He said, "Well, you know Jo's awfully lonely, and it would be nice if you would go there."

"David, I am not going to Mexico."

"Oh," he said, "I'm sorry, I guess I'll have to send him some movies."

Good friend that he was, he was worried about Jo being lonely in Mexico. Off he went, maybe to order some movies to be sent south of the border.

Rexy appeared. Actually, he appeared stunned. "Patricia, why didn't you tell me you were coming? I'd have picked you up. I thought you were working."

"I didn't know I was coming until the last minute," I lied.

"Look, Ma. No crutches." I stood up straight.

"Then, may I have this dance?"

"Hold me very tight, so I won't fall."

"You can depend on that," he said softly as he drew me to him.

So close did he hold me that we were not dancing, just standing, barely swaying to the music.

"I rather miss old Jo," said Rexy.

"Yes," I said softly.

"Still, we don't need him do we?"

I thought it better not to answer to that one.

"No, we don't need him," repeated Rexy, stroking my back and living up to his name (which everyone knows is "Sexy Rexy"). . .the music stopped.

I moved away in search of Jennifer who was laughing wickedly.

I went home a little earlier than usual, since I was driving myself. Back in the Chateau Marmont, I thought . . . and I thought. Of course, I did miss Jo dreadfully, and I was rather alarmed at this sudden feeling. It upset me quite a bit.

Before he left for Mexico, he had telephoned me from his house and said he would write.

"I should like that," I said.

"How much would you like it?"

Slight pause. "Very much."

"In that case, I'll write you a little every day after I've finished shooting."

"Thank you."

"Patricia. . ."

"Don't say it," I interrupted.

"All right, not yet," he said and he hung up the telephone.

Why did I ask him not to say it? Was it because I thought he was going to say that he was falling in love with me? Probably. And, why was I so afraid of hearing it? Because I would have to answer him.

During the months that he and Rex had been on either side of me, with my crutches as we went to the Selznicks', I had begun to lean a little closer to Jo because it gave me a warm feeling that was dangerously close to becoming all consuming and I wanted to be even closer. But I was afraid I'd become too involved and that was not my plan. I was relieved when they dropped me home and went on their way.

Jo would take Rex to his house then go to his own home and telephone me! We would have a friendly conversation and then say goodnight. But, now that he was going away for quite a while, he was bold enough to try and tell me the truth. I was not sure or ready to answer him . . . so, I delayed the inevitable.

* * *

I received a beautiful letter from him. It seems he had been trying to telephone me and telephone calls from Mexico were very, very difficult from his location.

He was, however, away in Mexico for several months. He was being directed by that marvelous director Robert Aldrich, with whom I had worked some time ago, so, I thought he'd be happy on the picture. I was glad to hear that he wasn't too happy!

One day, I got a telephone call. It was from Mexico City. It was Jo.

"Bob has given me four days off," he said. "They're shooting some scenes without me, so I'm coming back. I haven't got time to talk because I'm just changing planes, but I arrive at 7:25 P.M. I, eh . . ." Click. He was cut off.

I didn't say anything. I didn't say, "Hello, Jo." I didn't say, "Goodbye, Jo." I didn't say, "How nice you're coming back." I did not say anything.

But at 7:25 P.M., I found myself at Los Angeles airport sitting in my motor car.

A lot of people came out. I tried to look inconspicuous and I think I succeeded.

A tall, thin straight figure appeared. He seemed about to call a taxi but he turned. I saw his beautiful head outlined against the coming darkness. He looked directly at me.

As I met his look, I knew perfectly well that I was in love with him.

He slipped easily beside me and we drove off to my apartment.

We did not say one word during the entire drive from the Airport to the Chateau Marmont, and it was quite a long drive. I felt him look at me occasionally, but he did not attempt to speak. Somehow, there was a spell that we both needed to digest before daring to break it.

I parked the car and we got into the elevator rather as if we had never met.

I unlocked the door, dropped my handbag in a chair and walked over to the window with my back to him.

I was scared, not of him, but of me. I knew that our next move, which was becoming more and more inevitable, would have to be a commitment — a commitment that I had not wanted, had been able to avoid for so many self-sufficient years — yet, I had driven him here, to my apartment.

He walked up to me, turned me round to face him.

"Patricia, I love you deeply and I want you to marry me. You know that, don't you?"

"Please don't discuss marriage."

He looked at me and said very quietly, "Does marriage scare you?"

Equally quietly, I said, "Yes."

"Do I scare you?"

"No."

"That's a relief."

I turned and half faced him. He gave me a gentle, very sensitive and understanding smile, and then in a totally different voice he said, "Why don't we go out and have dinner? I'll tell you about Mexico and you can tell me all your news."

Eternally mine.

He didn't have to wait for an answer.

"I'll just go and freshen up," he said, as he went into the bathroom.

He came out looking so terribly attractive, so elegant in a clean shirt, an ascot that only he should wear, and a jacket that fitted his over-straight back perfectly.

If he was tired from the work and the journey (which he must have been), it didn't show at all.

We walked to the corner where Frascati's was at the time. They gave us a little table in the corner at the back. He ordered some wine. We sipped a glass each.

"Now, Patricia, you first. What have you been doing while I was in Mexico?"

"Missing you," I gulped my wine and got up. "Let's go," I said.

He paid the bill and followed me out. As we started to walk, he put his arm around me. We kissed, a few more steps and we kissed again.

I handed him the key to my apartment. We had already wasted too much time.

* * *

Sooner than he'd supposed he had to return and finish the picture in Mexico.

I missed him much too much.

He then had to go to England to dub it.

Well, I didn't go to Mexico when David asked me to because I wasn't going to be a "camp follower," and, I just couldn't go to my own country *now* because I would still feel like a "camp follower," even there.

While he was there he called on my mother and father whom he'd met while they were out here at a Selznick luncheon party. They enjoyed seeing him, and on our weekly telephone call, Mummy said, "I'm sure you're not surprised at who was here today . . . Joseph Cotten."

I said, "Oh, really, Mummy. How nice."

She said, "Yes, dear. I think it's very nice. In fact, I think we'll be seeing quite a lot of him!"

Mummy is a very evil woman. She is so straightforward and I love her very much, but she really does jump the gun. Maybe she didn't at all, maybe she was absolutely accurate . . . maybe!

* * *

When Jo came home, he asked me to marry him as if he'd never mentioned it before. I said that I had no intention of marrying again, that this whole thing had thrown me into a tizzy, and, yes, I did love him, but I didn't know whether marriage would work at all.

He assured me it would. He thought we'd better go up and have a talk with David Selznick, whom he always went to when he had a problem. He could solve our problem.

David was standing by the fire as we walked in.

"What's the problem, Jo?"

"I've asked Patricia to marry me."

"*That's* a problem?!" said David, aghast.

I felt like an idiot.

David said, "Come and sit here, Pat," he pointed to the sofa.

When I was seated he sat beside me and said, "I've often wondered why you haven't married again. I think you are determined not to make another mistake. Tell me, are you in love with Jo? He's obviously in love with you."

"Yes, I am in love with him, but it's such a shock. Why did it have to be Jo?"

"You're worried because you've known him so long and never as a single man? You feel it was another life?"

"Yes."

"But, my dear girl, *this* is another life. You and Jo have fallen in love and you have the kind of love neither of you has had before. I think you should cherish it and nourish it together. Simply put, Jo wants to marry you because he loves you. If you love him, as you say you do, then marry him and enjoy every minute you have together." David's serious face, at that moment, looked absolutely beautiful.

I stood up, and pecked David on the forehead, to his embarrassment. Then I went and sat by Jo, as close as I could get, and buried my head in his marvelous shoulder into which I shed a few tears.

Not only did David solve our problem, but my friend Jennifer, Jo's friend Jennifer — David's beautiful Jennifer — came out with the perfect solution.

"Get married in this house," which, of course, is what we did.

"And where are you going on your honeymoon?" said David.

"I'd like to go to England," I said.

"We're going to England," said Jo.

David walked over to me and said, "Congratulations, Pat." Then walked over to Jo, slapped him on the shoulder and said, "Good luck, Jo!"

What good friends! What a lovely wedding.

I asked David if he would give me away.

"I rather thought I would be Jo's best man."

Jennifer interrupted immediately, "David, you cannot play both parts. This is not a David O. Selznick production."

It became instead a Jennifer Jones' production. "Poor Pat hasn't got her father here. Jo have you anyone else you can use as your best man if Pat uses David, said our new producer.

"Patricia, since you need David desperately, I will call Francis Martin, my friend in San Francisco, and ask him to be my best man. I will not ask anyone else in Hollywood. David is my best friend."

Francis Martin and his wife, Nini, came and lent glamour to the occasion.

It had been decided that we would spend the night in the "Boys House" at the back of the Selznick property. It was called the "Boys House" because Jennifer and David's sons used it on many occasions. After our wedding night, it was renamed "Honeymoon Cottage."

However, before we made use of "Honeymoon Cottage," we went through a twilight ceremony. It wasn't a big wedding. Just a group of close friends (we did allow David and Jennifer to invite a few of theirs!).

* * *

I wouldn't see Jo the day before the wedding.

Jennifer was busy arranging the terrace. It was always beautiful, but she had it made even more beautiful.

The Reverend Dr. Wheatley, who was to perform the wedding, went to Jennie and David's house and rehearsed with Jo and Jennifer. Jennifer was worried about my too small feet on the little brick steps and David's too large ones. She and Jo apparently handled them very gracefully.

In our clumsy way, David got me to the altar.

Jo was trying to keep serious after I made a suggestive remark to him within the preacher's hearing distance. It had just become a legal suggestion!

* * *

Among our friends who attended were Dorothy Maguire and her husband, renowned photographer John Swope. As we would not have the press (only close friends), John took some lovely pictures. Producer Bill Frye came with associate producer James Wharton. Also, in attendance were actor Brian Aherne and his Eleanor; Ruthie and Carl Esmond; Lennie Gersch; producer/director Freddie de Cordova, who brought a carload with him; Joe Rock, who produced my first, awful screen test in England; Jean Howard; Dominick Dunne and his wife Lennie (Dominick has since then become a very famous author and journalist); Collier Young; General Frank McCarthy; Nini and Francis Martin (our best man); and Mary Jennifer was the little flower girl.

I do remember that we were married on the same day that Clifton Webb's mother's funeral took place. Many of the same guests attended both affairs. Since Mabel Webb's funeral was in the morning and our wedding was in the evening, I told our lot to change clothes. With all due respect to Clifton and Mabel, I thought it better that the guests didn't attend our vows in funeral attire.

* * *

We were married on the terrace. The minister had his back to a beautiful glowing fire. Two white cockatoos in their cage were to the right of the fireplace. They didn't make a sound during the ceremony, just sat perched with their heads as close as could be, as if they were committing to each other.

The million votive candles from the Boys' House to the terrace flickered in the breeze.

David Selznick gave me to Jo. Francis Martin produced the ring. We said our vows and the Rev. Dr. Wheatley pronounced us man and wife.

As we stood in the house, after the ceremony, waiting to greet the guests (the Reverend first and all the others behind him), Jo couldn't take his eyes off me. "You look like an angel," he said softly.

I looked straight at his handsome face with my most unangelic eyes and said, equally softly, "If you play your cards right, I'll go to bed with you tonight."

"Congratulations," said the Rev. Dr. Wheatley to Jo, who was still trying to control his reaction to my remark.

* * *

When we ran to our cottage, we were followed by the orchestra quite far behind us playing "I'll Be Loving You Always." A prediction. The music faded away as we opened the door, found a magnum of champagne and two glasses tied with white ribbons. There were little dainty sandwiches in each room.

Jennifer had not forgotten anything.

* * *

The following morning, we had a limousine pick us up very early to take us to Los Angeles airport.

On the airplane, we snuggled in the two very front seats. I was a little cold, so Jo called for the stewardess.

"Could you bring another blanket for my wife?" he said.

I pulled his face down to mine and said, "That's the first time you have called me your wife."

* * *

We were greeted by my entire family at the airport.

Jo, of course, knew Mummy and Daddy, but he hadn't met Piti and Ken, or Gloria and Gerry. All the press were there and Gloria was trying to contain her laughter because the press asked Piti, "What do you think the first thing Mr. and Mrs. Cotten will do on arriving in England?"

Piti quite sensibly answered, "Go to bed, I suppose."

That broke Gloria up, and Piti was very cross with her because she said, "After that long a journey what else would they do?"

Even Mummy had to try and hide her smile at that. But Piti accused them of having evil minds.

So you see what Jo fell into!

He became part of the family immediately.

* * *

I had taken an apartment which the Nivens had had while he made a film in England. I asked them to keep it on and we'd take it.

We had this very nice apartment on Eton Place. It had four bedrooms. Three of which I walked through once.

But nobody telephoned me. I wanted to talk to Mummy, I wanted to talk to Piti and Gloria but nobody telephoned me.

* * *

One night, after we'd been there close to a week, I got up and walked to the window. Jo got up too and came close beside me. He stroked my hair and looked at the sky. Then he said, "Patricia, why don't you call your mother in the morning? They know we're on our honeymoon and I think they're being very tactful. Why don't you call her and meet them all for lunch? You must have a lot to talk about, a lot of things you don't want me to hear." He turned me round, kissed me tenderly and led me back to bed.

He was right. They were being tactful. Mummy had called them and told everyone not to get in touch with me.

"You know how you all go on. He's very nice to have brought her here, and we must wait until she calls us."

Well, thanks to Jo, I did call them. We had a wild lunch and I talked about my husband, and they talked about my husband and how much they liked him. We had so much fun.

Jo and I had fun alone. We went to the theatre. We had dinner in little restaurants. We walked down Bond Street. We went to Harrods. We did as much of the city as we could, but sometimes we just went back to our rented flat, and behaved like two people on their honeymoon.

Piti and Ken were going to Paris on business. Suddenly, Jo said," Why don't we get on the train with them? They can go on about their business and we can start Europe in Paris."

So — the four of us got on the night train to Paris. They did what they had to do, and we did what we wanted to do.

Jo and Ken became great friends. In fact, they became like brothers, which was fine with us because the three of us were close sisters, and now we had a brother. (I should like to make it quite clear that Piti and Gloria had a brother. There was nothing fraternal about my relationship with Jo!)

* * *

At any time of one's life, Paris is, without a doubt, one of the most beautiful of all cities. If you go there alone, it is beautiful. If you are with friends, it is beautiful. If you have been there often, you are surprised each time by its beauty. But, when you go there on your honeymoon, you become involved in the magic that penetrates the air.

From the Eiffel Tower to the Champs Elysees, from Montmartre to the Left Bank, and even from the decadence of the Follies Bergere to the purity of the Louvre and the silence of Notre Dame, all these wonders envelop you so completely that it is you who are beautiful.

The city became a backdrop, fading in the knowledge that we had come to *own* Paris while we were there. We accepted all that it had to offer, and, in those surroundings, loved each other to the fullest until we took our love elsewhere.

This proud and arrogant land, respects and bows only to lovers — so we said, *"Vive la France,"* and we left for Venice.

* * *

Jo couldn't believe that in all my travels I had never been to Venice. He was overjoyed at being able to introduce me to it. How well I can understand that feeling.

We sailed into the Gritti Palace Hotel and had a twilight dinner on the terrace. It was so peaceful. We didn't feel like eating much — Jo was tired with excitement and I with anticipation.

We dragged our weary legs outside, and, without noticing, we were in a gondola being serenaded! The Gondolier made himself invisible, apparently by force of habit, while we unabashedly kissed, looked at the stars and whispered sweet nothings to each other.

Finally, we went back to the hotel. Jo said the next day would be special — we had such a short time before going on to Greece.

After early croissants and coffee, we went for a walk. He seemed to be steering me through all the little, narrow winding streets; they were old and picturesque and a little claustrophobic. It was dark and I wondered why these little streets were chosen for our walk.

Suddenly . . . oh, so very suddenly, Jo asked me to close my eyes. He held my hand and slowly we came to a stop.

"Open your eyes, darling."

I stood gazing at St. Mark's Square and burst into tears. The vastness, the strong light from

Heaven made me stagger and hang onto Jo while I drank it all in through my tears: The Doge's Palaces; all the surrounding buildings; the little restaurants on each side; the million pigeons that seemed to be moving in time with the music.

Jo found a table and we sat down. I hadn't said a word. Talking seemed almost sacrilegious.

Silently, I said a little prayer of gratitude. Jo knew how I felt and I included him in my prayer.

Paris had been so beautiful, so sophisticated — even slightly fearful with its ever-lasting sensuality. Venice was, by comparison, naive, gentle and languid — holding back, asking you to treat its romance as incomplete . . . a prelude to the next visit.

* * *

In Greece, we, of course, had to go to the Acropolis. It was raining and I was wearing high heels. We got soaked and returned to the hotel.

I led Jo to the window of our suite from whence we had the most beautiful view of the Acropolis. I told Jo that was the only way to see it.

When it stopped raining, we took off again round Athens, looking at the shops and searching for little restaurants.

A young man, a student, I think, chased us for quite a long way and stopped Jo for an autograph. He was very excited, and Jo shook his hand. The young man said, "Mr. Cotten, I admire your films so much, but what a pleasure it is to see you in the bones."

I told Jo it was so good that he hadn't seen Orson "in the bones," which suited Jo as much as "in the flesh." He was always slim. All 6 feet 2 inches of him.

I was impressed with the country but slightly homesick. Jo was my understanding, my permanent oasis. He knew what I was thinking without my having to tell him.

After the cleanliness and the foreignness of Greece, interesting, strange and eclectic but seemingly without fault, Turkey was opulent, noisy and buzzing with life. Honesty was the reality that cloaked dishonesty. Unlike Greece, which seemed faultless, Turkey enjoyed its faults — those that were unhidden.

The people we met, we liked. Of course, I am, in a few words, giving my opinionated opinion on very short visits to these famous countries. I was on my honeymoon and I deemed nor felt any criticism. So, I wallowed in my geographical lack of knowledge. An amateur bride clinging only to love. Therefore, as Shakespeare said, "The rest is silence . . . "

* * *

We finally went back to England to say *au revoir* to them all.

We came home via Virginia to see Jo's family on our final honeymoon stop.

From New York we went by train to Washington, then we rented a car to go to Richmond to spend the night with Jo's cousin Ria and her husband before going on to Petersburg to see Jo's mother and brothers.

I was staggered during the drive from Washington to Virginia. Never ever have I seen such strong violent colors. The trees were a brilliant red — I had not seen such a red on any living thing — sometimes mixed with a daffodil yellow, and, interrupting these two colors, a real orange; the color of oranges. No crazy, brilliant artist could leave such strong alive colors on his palette. Together, Lautrec, Manet, Van Gogh, Monet, Cezanne, Picasso, Modigliani and many others with a huge canvas would not channel their colors to emulate the Virginia scenery.

The occasional green of many trees seemed to attract birds who also had the temerity to flaunt their rainbow wings as they flew from tree to tree singing the song of Southern nature.

We arrived in Richmond late. His cousin Ria and Fred, her husband, have a lovely estate in Richmond. They gave us a wonderful welcome, embracing us both strongly. This, I thought to myself, will be the most restful and cozy evening; we can just sit and talk happily amid all this beauty.

Ria greeted me with a long speech — I did not understand a single word she said! Aside from the strongest Southern accent imaginable, she had an unfortunate speech defect! Impossible to know what to do . . . when she smiled, I smiled. When she laughed, I laughed. She hugged me occasionally and, of course, I returned the hugs, *but* it was the most exhausting strain-filled evening I think I have ever been through. Finally, I admitted to a terrible headache which I had had for some time. So, excusing myself, I ran upstairs, took two aspirin and flung myself on the bed. I heard Jo say (and I understood him - thank heavens!), "I'd better go up and be with her. She's had a very tiring day."

When he came up and shut the door, I was near tears. "Why didn't you warn me?" I almost screamed.

He tried not to chuckle but couldn't resist lying on the bed and tears of laughter streamed down his face. "Oh, darling, if you could have seen your face. Of course, I should have thought to warn you, but we are all so used to it. I don't know why I thought you knew. I'll help you all I can and never leave you alone with her. I'll always be there to translate for you." He turned his head and couldn't hide his laughter. Apparently, it was my reaction that caused all the hilarity!

The following day, we borrowed Fred's Rolls and drove through the glory that was Virginia to Petersburg. I loved Jo's mother immediately, sweet and gentle with a slight, soft Southern accent. Her smile was beautiful and her still-beautiful eyes spoke worlds.

"Do you find me difficult to understand, Patricia?" she asked.

"No, Mother Cotten. I understand every word you say. However, I can't understand a word Ria says. I must confess, I do find her speech very difficult."

Jo's mother put her arm round me and said, "We all do, my dear. Just smile and tune her out. When you're used to it, you'll be just like all of us — "

Mother Cotten was really old, but bright and brave and I loved her very much. She always called me "God's perfect child." It made Jo so happy. Me too!

Editor's Note:

I couldn't resist persuading Patricia to allow her book to include a small portion of Jo's many, many letters he wrote to her during the three months he was filming *"The Last Sunset"* in Mexico. This was before they were married, how could she not fall in love with him.

The letters are so sincere and poetic, you, the reader, will have an even greater understanding of his beautiful soul, his humor and, of course, his intense love for her.

Friday.

My darling: Thank you for your sweet, adorable letter which you wrote on Sunday, and which got here yesterday, and which I opened with the indifference of a parched prospector coming upon a water hole in Death Valley.

Half of your wish has already come true. I am, indeed, miserable, my darling Patricia. I haven't been so lonesome, so homesick, so heartsick, so utterly lost since I went to summer camp with the St. John's P.E. Boys Brigade on the muddy James River in 1898.

Harriet Aldrich was on the set today, and I discovered that she is a cross-word addict. I was delighted because it gave me an opportunity to say your name outloud. I mentioned, I'm afraid in a terribly fake-casual manner, that you too loved cross-words. And with great restraint did not add that I too love you. Which, by the way, I do.

J.

Wednesday.

My Darling: The second day of this wretched picture is not yet over, and to me it seems to have been running longer that "Abie'sIrish Rose."

I've been at it again-sleeping. I finished work early today, came home and had the world's greatest nap, and after more than nine hours last night. I don't believe it's particularly because I'm so far behind in rest, since fatigue is not accumulative, they say. (Though who "they" are I do not know) I rather think I sleep, hoping to escape the unhappiness of being away from you, hoping perhaps to awaken and find myself out of this unreal bondage and in you arms. Alas, I open my eyes only to another black chapter of an endless nightmare. Is there such a thing as excessive love? If so, is it dangerous?

J.

Friday.

My darling: It gets worse as I feel closer to you, and I feel closer to you everyday in my heart, and I know everyday I must be closer to that damned airport, which I hated the last time I saw it, and which will represent complete happiness to me when I next see it. We must never, never be apart like this again, Patricia darling. I don't even know where you are tonight, nor at what attending admirer to aim my envy and radio-active curses. I shall be obliged to save those and send them all tomorrow in the direction of the charmer, in the hope that they execute him before you are called up to say "no---" my only answer- Oh how I suffer when I think of anyone, anyone else making love to you, touching you- you having to discuss even in negative terms their desire for you or being anywhere near another's rapture, physical or otherwise. I love you, my darling, and want you nowhere ever except very close to me. I thought tonight how much we together would have enjoyed an evening that was simply minute-counting for me. Bendiccio turned out to be a most interesting man in a fascinating house and studio, and though his paintings were much too abstract for my absent thoughts, his theory of geometrics in art did persuade me that they were born of a deep conviction and certainly could not have been expressed in his conception by Joseph Cotten. It led me to think that perhaps there is existing in the creative world too much theory. I consider this; that I came to the horrible conclusion that I was making a theory on the subject of antitheorism. I think I don't have any theories about us. Theory, it seems to me is subject to change- and love and respect, I imagine, have always been constant, and always will be. Actually, I don't care much about seeing the heiresses house, as curious as I am about it, because my interests in anything at all are only empty fillers without you to share them with me, discuss them with me, and laugh about them with me.

I miss you so dreadfully darling, and I love you so very much. Goodnight.

J.

Sunday morning.

My darling: Another day is on its way to ending this endless separation from the only one in the world who means anything to me. I've just been swimming, and experienced something new. It's the first time I've ever missed anyone under water.

I'm going to lunch now, and I'll either finish this in Mexico, or mail it when I get there if it's late.

It's just to say to you, to remind you of something. That space denies me the privilege of doing in person-that I love you deeply, my darling, darling one.

J.

Years later.but.still Thursday.

My Darling: I've been pondering in the pantry (really have) and wondering what corrupts us to expand, to elaborate on the system of things in which we are often happily placed. Damned decision, damned ambition, damned necessity.

Now that my understamped letters are getting to you, the over-stamped ones are probably arriving at the same time, and you are sated with words from me.

I love you, my Patricia-

J.

P.S. Your Monday note came today-and from our telephone conversation, I realize with horror that I am to expect no more because of my uncertain departure from here. Believe me, my darling, you have no monopoly on internal sobbing, which you wrote about so sweetly, but alas, too briefly and much, much too infrequently.

I.L.Y.

Tuesday.

My darling! Your two telegrams came yesterday, easing my pain, and your silence after so much misunderstanding and bewilderment.

I am booked out of here on the Sat. night train-Mex. City Sunday morning, Los Angeles about 2:30 Sunday-barring more breakdowns caused by wind, dust, clouds, rain, mules and electricity. The assistant thinks I can't make it until Monday night from here, but I'm sticking with great hope and determination to my PR schedule.

Darling, darling, darling. I miss you to a degree of absolute complete distraction. I sit in a glassy-eyed stupor thinking of nothing else, and awaken in black dejection when I realize how far away you are.

I love you, my beautiful, darling Patricia-

Tuesday-7:30

My darling: I'm so glad I called, and found you there this evening. I was so hurt, so dismally lonely, that I had persuaded myself that you had told me not to call you. I know truly that you hadn't said any such thing. And your voice and your words made me as close to feeling joyous as I can under these painful circumstances. We simply must not do these cruel things to each other. Please, darling, know that I will never hurt you, will never take advantage of any degree of feelings you might have or might develop for me. I cherish your love more than anything, anything; and I want to keep it selfishly forever.

My cell-mate Tooney just called and I shall dine with and listen to him. He wasn't at all sure of tomorrow's plans, and since I haven't yet received a call sheet, I don't dare make a guess about the future. If I don't work tomorrow, I'm afraid that means a Saturday departure is hopeless. It's maddening, in spite of the fact that when I left Aguascalientes I was prepared for a this week return. I think at that time I would have agreed to anything in exchange for a flight into your arms.

Darling, know that I love you and that I have loved you for a long time. Know that I want to be with you, just you, and know that I suffer without you, suffer terribly. To hurt you slightly is the thing I most want to avoid, and I believe I can avoid it, and will.

I love you-

J.

Wednesday.

My darling: On my way home tonight I hopefully stopped by the Dan Marcos for the mail and brought home an armful for my three cell-mates. I don't feel the self-pity, the torture of loneliness much anymore,- there is just a numbness inside which makes me weak and sick and desolate. I suppose there is a merciful absorption point to this kind of pain and loneliness and perhaps I have reached it. Or perhaps it is because I try to condition myself (when I go there to the office every evening) by saying over and over that there will be no letter from you! but hoping, hoping so desperately that I am wrong. Darling, darling Patricia. I am so very hungry for a tender word from you.

I was given two small opportunities to talk about you today. Bob Aldrich, whom you have completely charmed, told me about the television show you did together, and the dialogue director, Bob Sherwood, I think, wrote a "Rawhide" for you once.

It looks now as if I can't leave until Monday, although I'm still hoping for Saturday. I shan't give up hoping until Friday and I'll wire you then. If it has to be Monday, it will mean, at least, that I'll have two more days at the other end of my trip- maybe more, the way we're now falling behind.

While there may be an absorption point to those black emotions I mentioned, there is, happily, no such governor of love. And while it may be true about absence not being a stimulant for love, mine for you, my darling Patricia, grows deeper, more absorbing everyday; and while I am absorbed by it apparently, the boundaries of it are ever increasing. Oh, how I do, to borrow a phrase, need you.

I love you-

J.

- 12 -

And We Found Paradise

When we got married, Jo put the house that he had owned during his former marriage on the market. Both he and I wanted a place of our own. While we were on our honeymoon, it sold, which made me very happy because going to live in that house just didn't feel right to me.

However, a few days before we came back from Virginia, we received a telegram from the agent saying the deal had fallen through. So, my darling Jo said, "Let's take a bungalow at the Beverly Hills Hotel, and leave it on the market. When we sell it, we'll buy a house especially for you."

I agreed to that and I telephoned my mother about our plans.

She said, "I think you're being very childish. The house may take a while to sell and Jo apparently loves it. He chose it. You can give it your touch and it would be all right for the two of you. Living in a hotel is not a very good start for a marriage."

I took Mummy's advice and I said, "Jo, let's not go to a hotel. We'll move into your house in the Pacific Palisades, but I don't want to sleep in the master bedroom. We could be happy together in one of the guest rooms. We'll stay in a hotel for a week or so while you call the staff and have it changed around to make it suit us."

He said, "Darling Patricia, I don't think you really want to do this."

I said, "I do. I absolutely do. We can be together, we love each other, we'll leave it on the market, but until it sells, we shouldn't let silly 'school girl' feelings upset us."

So, we moved into the house, into the first guest room. It was very beautiful and we were happy.

* * *

One day when Jo was out working, I walked around the house. It was a huge five-story house with a fabulous view of the ocean. I walked all through it and I opened the door to the master bedroom and walked inside. It was completely empty. He had got rid of all the furniture. It wasn't anyone's room.

I thought, "Mummy was right. We'll have difficulty selling this. It's too big for most people; maybe Jo will let me have it all redecorated and it will become 'mine.'"

When he came home, I asked him.

He said, "Would you really like to do that?"

I said, "Yes I would."

"Do anything you like, paint it inside and outside, change everything, but only if that's really what you want."

I said that it was, but, we kept the house on the market.

We had it painted outside and inside. We got a lot of pieces of furniture that we both liked *and* I had an indoor pool put in what used to be the second drawing room, with three Venetian chandeliers hanging over it. The whole room was mirrored with gold leaf 'fleur de lys' panels. It became quite, quite beautiful. I added all my strong colors: turquoise, purple and hot pink cushions. Jo liked them too.

As well as being an actor and a gardener, Jo was a builder, an engineer and an all-around designer. (He loved to build six-foot walls.)

The pool was downstairs, so we had to have a hole in the house, a large hole, and for quite some time, so the men could get through with ladders and jackhammers and all their digging tools. Jo loved having a project, and, aside from the amazing Corinth Canal, this project was certainly the most ambitious.

He did a superb job supervising everything and making the electricity work, such as having the heating and cooling function perfectly without ever steaming up the mirrors.

He and Guy Womack, a friend and fine talented workman, put a white and gold flecked tile deck around the pool. They put heavy paper all over it until it dried.

I rushed in to admire their work and ran along the paper where it overlapped the pool and I fell backwards, fully dressed into the water, thereby unintentionally christening it.

* * *

It was a "show place" that was "almost" mine. We gave many parties, for it was indeed on the market for a long time. Mostly, we gave Sunday lunches in the summer overlooking the Pacific Ocean. We had the usual group of friends: Jennifer and David, Veronique and Gregory Peck, Ruthie and Carl Esmond and the fine writer, Ivan Moffat. When Brits were in town, of course, I invited them — Larry Olivier, David and Hjordis Niven and Gladys Cooper (the wonderful English actress with so much personality). We had evening parties, too, and we always had music.

Few people came to look at the house. We got out quickly before they came and left it to John, the butler, to show them round.

One of the people who made an appointment to see the house was Mae West. We were rather happy about that. We thought she'd fall in love with that wonderful pool and have some marvelous parties there. She could fill the pool with young men and her own voluptuous self.

We left the house about half an hour before she was due to arrive and stayed away for quite a while. We went for a long and hopeful drive.

On returning, we couldn't wait to ask John about the encounter.

"John," I said, "what happened with Miss West? How did she like the house?"

He looked at me rather furtively and said, "Well, she came to the door with a young man whom she was holding by the arm closely, I thought he was her chauffeur, but she seemed very affectionate toward him.

"I opened the door and said, 'Good afternoon, Miss West.'

"She said, 'Where's the master bedroom?'

"'Upstairs,' I said.

"'Too far,' was her response as she turned around and left.

"She didn't even step over the threshold."

Poor John was quite stunned. Jo and I laughed enormously.

Jo said, "Suppose his answer had been — 'The master bedroom is right here.' What do you think she'd have said?"

"Nothing," I replied. Of course, she might have dismissed him and gone inside to try it out!

"Oh, poor John," said Jo. "He probably had been looking forward to showing her round the place listening to that inimitable 'voice.'"

It wasn't a voice really, just a sexual murmur that had proven very profitable in more ways than one. Obviously, she never would have made it to the pool — it was downstairs!

Well, that was that.

However, some years later we did sell the house to a young couple. They were going to give a big party and they wanted to move in very soon, which they did. We got out, and left a lot of things for them. When I found out some time later that Jo had practically "given" them the house, I should have been shocked. But you see, I had fallen passionately in love with Jo before I married him. After our honeymoon, I realized that not only was he physically perfect, he was generous to a fault — gentle, intelligent with the most unique dry wit (I had witnessed some of that before) and that wherever we lived I had to have him near me. We loved each other completely, but, most importantly, we respected each other. How could I have found it all — while looking the other way.

* * *

We decided not to buy another house but to look at condominiums. We were now beginning to travel a great deal. Jo was getting movie offers from Italy, Spain and France. Always we stayed a while in England en route.

One year we had used our original house for four days in a whole year. It seemed much wiser to have an apartment and just lock the door and leave. We had lost our dog which had broken our hearts. No, we shouldn't own a house, and we shouldn't have a pet. We were becoming gypsies and we couldn't take a pet on our travels, especially not to England because of the quarantine.

We travelled to England on the last trip the Queen Mary took. It was sad that it was her final voyage, but memorable. No ship that we have been on since can compared to the old Queen Mary.

We came back from England to New York on the Concorde (I think it was her second trip). I was a bit nervous about the speed but Jo loved it, and he held my hand as we crossed the sound barrier.

* * *

We took a bungalow at the Chateau Marmont (from where I had left to marry), and we looked at apartments.

We looked at a dream penthouse. I had to wait in the car for Jo while he gave the key back.

"Which one shall we look at next?" I said.

"None," said my husband.

"Well, we have two others to look at."

"No, we don't. That penthouse is ours."

"What do you mean?"

"Patricia, I saw the expression on your face and I have just been inside arranging for us to move in next week."

I stared at him with shining eyes as he said, "It's yours darling."

* * *

Moving in there was like a second honeymoon, or a second/ first, really.

My dear mother's advice, which had always been infallible, was for once wrong. She told me with the best of intentions for both of us that it would be childish to stay in a hotel instead of moving into the former house. Perhaps, she had forgotten that a woman in love *is* childish, possessive, and oh so sensitive.

I had tried at great expense, financially and emotionally, to change it all, but the house didn't change. I began to change. Not deep inside, but my personality lost its natural vitality and I became physically frail — real or imagined — and a shadow of my former self existed in those rooms. It did not affect my love for Jo, but I began to lose confidence in myself and I didn't know the reason.

Dr. Forde and Jo sensed that I was in the wrong world and my darling Jo immediately set about making it right. Against all my protests, he cleared the decks and we moved out.

When he saw the expression on my face as I looked around the apartment, my vitality returned.

"It's yours, darling," he repeated.

Yes, it was mine. The walls, the carpets, the ceilings, the view — they all seemed to be singing a welcoming song.

I waved my hand with an imperious gesture, telling Jo that the huge terrace was his. "You can fill it with all your favorite flowers."

On the terrace in our apartment. It was huge and overlooked all of Los Angeles. The painting behind Jo, I did. In between Jo's flowers and trees, I hung one of my paintings. It was our outside room.

He didn't look at the lovely terrace. He just stared at me with such pride and said, "Since I go with the territory, Patricia darling, will you be my wife?"

"Yes, please. I thought you'd never ask."

He smiled and took my hand as we walked through the rooms together.

"I am now going to wallow in my new bathtub and I shall come out smelling sweeter than all your exotic flowers."

I reappeared smelling of jasmine and wearing a shocking-pink chiffon nightdress with very thin spaghetti straps. Jo was standing in the bedroom in a silk bathrobe. It was a cold night.

"Shall I turn the heating on?" I asked in my most wifely way.

"No," he replied. "We won't need it." Walking over to me, he delicately slipped each strap off my shoulders, the nightdress fell silently to the floor.

As he lay me on the bed, he whispered, "This apartment is yours. You have told me you love it. That's so good to know. You, my darling, are mine. In case you don't realize how much I love you, I intend to show you."

My darling husband knew, or at least felt it incumbent on himself, to teach (as he may have thought) me every beautiful, daring, exciting and almost uncontrollable way in which to show me what love could be. Violent yet gentle. Interminable but with a promise of repetition in an even slightly different way. Immediate or later — there had been no beginning and there could be no ending.

"Patricia, my darling, I do love you," he murmured.

And, for the first time in my life, I said, "And I love you, too."

Everything faded as he passionately kissed me and made love to me again. It was slow and gentle and tantalizing, and when he could tease me no longer, his loving became implicit and together we reached another dimension and died a little.

We had not turned on the heating.

We did not go to sleep.

* * *

We hadn't been there long when I was sent a script which was to be made in Salt Lake City. I was lying on the sofa in the living room reading it.

Jo came in and said, "Bob Sherr told me he was sending you a script. How is it?"

"It's terribly good," said I, honestly. "Really extremely good."

He wandered off and a little while later he came in and said, "How is the part?"

"It's the best part I've been offered. It's absolutely me."

He stroked my head and said, "Oh, good."

After I finished reading it, I telephoned Bob Sherr, my agent, and said, "Bob, it's a great script and a great part, but I'm not going to do it. In fact, I'm not going to do any work that takes me away from my husband. We don't have to work together *but* we have to live together. I can't be in Salt Lake City or anywhere if he's working somewhere else."

Jo passed by as he heard me say the last sentence. He took me in his arms and said, "thank you."

I didn't realize how very often, and for such a long time, I would hear him say "thank you," for anything at all that I did. Yet, that was my husband.

- 13 -

Almost Always in the Sky

Of course, we had to live together because very soon after that conversation, Jo had to start a picture at Twentieth Century Fox with Bette Davis and Joan Crawford called *Hush, Hush Sweet Charlotte*. At the same time, I also started a picture with a skating champion named Carol Heiss. They were planning to make her into a new Sonia Henie. It was a movie about Snow White and the Three Stooges. I was the wicked queen.

We worked at the same studio and got home within an hour of each other, and started living like two actors together.

His picture went on longer than mine because Joan got quite sick. She eventually was not able to continue with the part.

Bette telephoned me and said, "Why don't you play the part, Pat?"

I was altogether wrong for it, and, of course, I wasn't offered it. But Bette liked me (in spite of my choice of evening dresses) and she wanted someone she liked to do the picture. However, the studio sensibly sent for Olivia de Havilland from France, and she played the part quite beautifully.

Snow White and the Three Stooges. *I am the wicked queen at the foot of the bed. The girl kneeling by the bed was Carol Heiss, the skater.*

* * *

On a Saturday night towards the end of *Charlotte,* Olivia de Havilland had a birthday, and as they had been friends since they worked together at Warner Brothers Studios, Bette decided to give a big party for her. She was giving it in a Japanese restaurant because Olivia had been born in Japan.

We all met at Bette's house for drinks and then boarded a large bus that she hired for the evening. Off we went, beautifully dressed and excited until we arrived at our destination where we had to remove our shoes. Jo wasn't too happy about taking his off because he couldn't put them on again without a shoe horn. However, this was a party and he joined in with the festive atmosphere knowing that he'd take them back in the bus in his hands — Bette would lend him a shoe horn at her house.

Now that we were shoeless, we had to sit on the floor to dine with our legs crushed under a long, flat table, Japanese style. There were at least 50 of us — all happy and hungry.

First came the raw fish! I was sitting in between Jo and Jimmy Woolf, the famous English producer who, you will remember, with his brother, John, had produced that very successful English movie called *Room at the Top.* Jimmy was a very good friend of mine. Since our teens, we had been pals. We enjoyed each other's company, be it in England or the United States. Jo had come to know him and liked him enormously. John, his brother, is also a very good friend. Jo worked for him twice in England and found him most talented. But John was not at this party — just Jo, Jimmy and I among the 50 or so others.

After the fish came cold sake, which seemed warmer than the fish.

Everyone seemed to be doing quite well with the thousands of other innumerable courses. The three of us were struggling and, occasionally, suffering.

The room became suddenly very quiet — I think Olivia was about to say a few words. Before she had time, Jimmy Woolf leaned across me and said to Jo in clear tones, "I can't help but wish she'd been born in Paris."

Just our half of the table heard him. They all gave a tumultuous laugh.

"Tell us the joke, please," said Olivia.

"Oh, we can't," said Jimmy. "Patricia just told an off-color story and Jo won't let her repeat it."

I gave Jimmy as hard a kick as I could with my shoeless foot — and broke a toe!

* * *

After Jo had finished *Charlotte,* producer Paul Gregory, who had done some wondrous work on the stage like *Don Juan in Hell,* and several other classics with Charles Laughton and Agnes Moorehead, came to see us with a play that he thought we both might be interested in doing.

We read the play. It had a few faults, and Jo had a lot of suggestions. We met the two writers; Levinson and Link were their names. When I went into our den to meet them, Jo said, "Darling, I want you to meet Mr. Loeb and Mr. Leopold." He kept his usual straight face.

They were very young and quite determined not to change a word of their script. Jo refused to take the play, without the few changes, to New York.

The play somehow seemed jinxed —

Paul had a marvelous revolving stage built which enabled us to go from scene to scene without closing the curtains. It's so much easier to follow a play when it flows without too many black outs.

But, during our dress rehearsal in San Francisco, I had to make an easy exit. Not being accustomed to revolving stages, I caught my left leg badly in the doors as it went round and had to be rushed to the hospital to have it attended to. It was very painful, but I was determined not to limp during our opening. I was playing Jo's mistress and Agnes Moorehead was his wife. Between us, we had decided that Jo would choke her to death and run away with me. Therefore, no limping mistress seemed very helpful in planning a murder.

Jo murdered Aggie just before my entrance and he pulled her behind the sofa where she lay dead —

Enter "The Mistress": I look behind the sofa and sway in horror (quite easy with a gimpy leg), rushing to Jo, my lover, to hide my face.

From behind the sofa came the loudest sneeze I've ever heard. (The carpet was new and Aggie was allergic to it.)

Big unintentional comedy murder!

However, we had an extremely successful tour and the play made a lot of money.

* * *

In Philadelphia, the two young fellows came back stage. They were very nice indeed. They said they realized there were a few mistakes; they now had more authority (the director had been very weak). They had joined the Writers' Guild or whatever one does to change a writer into an author. Maybe it comes from the word "authority." Anyway, Jo did not change his mind and go to New York. We had had a long tour and we were both ready to go home. We wished them luck.

Boy, did they ever get it, and did they ever deserve it. They turned out to be fine writers and were the fair-haired boys at Universal Studios.

Jo and I went home and carried on with our lives — our crazy, wonderful lives. How could I ever have considered not marrying him? I thank God often for making Jo change my mind.

* * *

Howard Erskine, a producer who had seen us in *Rx Murder* (the title Jo gave the play with which we toured). Gave birth to the series *Columbo.* Thomas Mitchell played a detective in our play named Columbo. Peter Falk made the series a tremendous success.

Anyway, Howard Erskine and playwright Joseph Hayes came round with a play written by Hayes called *Calculated Risk.* They wanted us to perform it on Broadway with Robert Montgomery directing. We read it. It was very well written. I didn't really like my part very much. I played Jo's wife. I preferred to play his mistress (on the stage, that is).

We went to New York about a month before rehearsals were to begin so we could learn our parts and be letter perfect on the first day of rehearsals. Jo's part was enormous. He went through it every day and was word perfect by rehearsal time.

We opened.

The *New York Times* gave us an absolutely wonderful review. Upstairs at Sardi's they read it. We all celebrated.

After our celebration, Jo said we had to stop and buy other papers because tomorrow we were going to have a great queue, a line around the box office. We were a *hit*.

We were not able to buy a paper — we were not able to buy any papers — for the newspapers had gone on strike and our wonderful review never came out.

Everything started to close. Fine plays by great authors with great actors all began to fold like a deck of cards — no ads with no newspapers.

My darling husband decided that he was not going to close. As he worded it, "I am too vain to close."

* * *

One day, he was saved by the bell. The telephone rang. It was a Mr. Rorimer, who was the Curator for the Metropolitan Museum. He remembered Jo and Jennifer working there in *Portrait of Jennie*. He said he had to introduce the Mona Lisa on television, as the painting had been lent to the New York World's Fair.

"Nobody knows who I am and I think it should be introduced by a well-known person. Would you introduce me and then the picture? Everyone knows who you are. And, oh, by the way — if you accept, it's a very lucrative offer."

Since Jo was at that time being P. T. Barnum, or a reasonable facsimile, his mind worked even faster than usual, and he replied in a very mellifluous voice, "I would be honored to introduce you Mr. Rorimer, but rather than a presumably large fee, I would like them to give me air time on TV." (He did not add, "to salvage our flagging play.")

* * *

He went on TV and did every television show imaginable. He mentioned the title of the play and the theatre where it was playing. He, of course, introduced the famous da Vinci work of art, and while so doing the director would say, "Mr. Cotten, stand a little closer to Mona."

Ever since the day that I was finally wise enough to marry Jo, whenever I was at any studio working, one of the crew would come to me and say, 'Pat, how is Mr. Cotten?'

Then, Jo would go to a studio and the assistant director would say, 'Mr. Cotten, how is Pat?'

At the time, I had suggested to Jo that we do a series called 'Mr. Cotten and Pat.'

So, Jo wasn't in the least surprised when the director had said, 'Mr. Cotten, stand a little closer to Mona.'

Jo said, 'Certainly. Would you like me to smile?'

He really felt like smiling because he knew our play would keep running.

He kept the play open for the entire season which included a 100-day newspaper strike. We were a miracle play. We were a happy company, and Jo was responsible.

* * *

After *Calculated Risk*, Paul Gregory signed us again to do a wondrous evening in the theatre. It wasn't a play, although it had a title. It was called *Seven Ways of Love,* and it was as if two people were on the stage living a dream. The couple were called Joseph and

Patricia and, in turn, we would recite poems, prose and articles covering the seven ways of love. Some of which were: *Love of Food; Love of Country; Love of War; Love of Nature*; and, of course, the last one was, *Love of A Man and A Woman.*

There was some comedy, which mainly consisted of our discussions with each other before the lights went out, then one light would shine on Jo and I would be seated upstage in the dark. Jo, with his unique voice, would go into a long, strong, tragic, yet almost armed dissertation of *Love of War* — scary, yet beautiful, because there was truth in it. There were tears mixed with applause. When he finished, the lights went out again and I came down-stage and went into a half-song/half-poem about *Love of Food.* It was called *Rare Roast Beef.* I discovered, after several performances, that if I swiveled my hips and did a bump on the last line, I would get laughter and applause. The lights dimmed and then Jo appeared, all six-foot-two, standing erect and proud, letting his voice take him into a stirring version of *Love of Country.* "Americans are always moving on . . ." he ended with a fine crescendo.

Jo and Jennifer Jones in Portait of Jennie. *They were both delightful. I have called her "Jennie" ever since I saw it.*

Jo put his head down and his hand on his heart, and, as the lights faded on him, I appeared seated on a tufted stool, and a pinkish light came upon me. Because as Jo was unable to hide his real love of country, I was enabled to let my pride overcome me in Rupert Brooke's "There is some corner of a foreign field that is forever *England*."

All our recitations had so much meaning. In between, we would become ourselves and discuss or argue about them. Paul Gregory referred to our conversations as "the glue" which gently segwayed into powerful, tender and well-known classics.

Jo, with immense energy, gave a rendition of *This Then Is Man*. Biased though I am, I cannot imagine anyone doing it better. I recited a poem by Edna St. Vincent Millay, and then we started reading the letters that the Brownings had written to each other. I was enthralled by the beauty of some of Robert Browning's letters — so much love, so much sadness. Perhaps if you love so deeply, you pay for it in your heart.

Actually, I am completely sure that the giving of love is a fulfilling, satisfying emotion. Only God knows if we have earned the right to go on loving ad infinitum.

* * *

I do remember one funny thing that happened during *Calculated Risk*.

We rented an apartment that belonged to Hume and Jessica Cronyn. A beautiful penthouse. We didn't start out there. We were at a hotel that a friend had recommended. Not a very nice hotel, but it had a large and lovely penthouse.

One morning, Jo got up before I did. I heard a thundering noise and knew there had been a terrible explosion somewhere in New York.

Jo came wading into our bedroom. "What happened?" I asked.

"Quick, put something on. Get up. The water tank on the roof has exploded and it will flood the whole building."

He got me a coat and he helped me through the water that was now filling our living room.

He said, "You get into this elevator as soon as it arrives." Always thinking, he added, "I'm going to talk to the police and see if they can open the street so we can get to the theatre as we have a matinee today."

He left me by the elevator and as soon as it opened, I jumped inside and he ran downstairs.

When the elevator doors closed, the roof caved in and an enormous amount of water—filthy, dirty water — came pouring all over me from head to foot. I was like a drowned rat.

When I arrived in the lobby there were a lot of people in their dressing gowns and with their hair curlers. All were half dressed. It was quite early, and there were cameras there — television cameras. Aside from flooding the elevator, neither the water nor the dirt affected its movement. We landed with a thud.

I came out, a poor drowned rat with dirty mud and straight hair hanging all over my face. A reporter spotted this apparition and said, "Oh, isn't that Patricia Medina? Come here, Miss Medina. You're in a play with your husband, Joseph Cotten. Would you like to say a few words?" and he pushed my face toward the camera.

I smiled right into the lens as if I really thought I looked like Elizabeth Taylor and said, "I'm sorry, I think I'm drowning."

"No, no. You're perfectly all right."

Now Jo came running in. Thank heaven!

"It's all right. Oh, are you all right?" He paled when he saw me.

"Yes."

"Well, eh — they're going to open the street for us and we can get through, hopefully to the theatre."

So I said, "What am I going to do about my hair? Look at this mess."

Dear Jo, he always looked at me as if I were perfectly beautiful, and I looked horrendous.

I said, "Look, if one of the firemen could go upstairs there is a wig in one of the drawers there and I could wear it for the matinee."

One of the men yelled out, "Would you go up to the Cottens' apartment and get Miss Medina's hairpiece?"

I didn't think that sounded too nice and I turned to the lady next to me to ask how she was.

She yelled out, lisping, "And while you're up there, go next door and get my teeth. They're in a glass by my bed!"

I think she got her teeth.

I know I got my wig, so we flew out out of the hotel onto the stage. Everybody had heard what had happened to our hotel.

Of course, every time we came on stage, we were greeted with enthusiastic applause, but this time, they clapped and yelled. It was worth the indignity that we'd been through. They seemed so glad that we were there, and so were we.

When we finished the play, we returned to California. We'd begun to rather like apartment living after staying in the Cronyn's lovely place.

* * *

We were very happy in our new apartment with its enormous terrace that Jo filled with trees and flowers.

We still had our good friends that had come to our wedding, but as long as we had each other . . . how complete we were.

Jo was offered a picture in England with Katharine Hepburn. We left about a month early and took a seven-year lease on an apartment on Mount Street in London. It was just what we wanted, with its lovely Adams' fireplace in the drawing room. Everything seemed perfect for us. We furnished it almost in a day and moved in just about a week before Jo was to begin Edward Albee's *A Delicate Balance* with Katharine Hepburn and Paul Scofield. With those two actors, he had a wonderfully happy time.

Jo was delighted to be working with Katharine again. He had played with her many years before in *The Philadelphia Story.* She rented a house round the corner from our apartment.

She said to Jo, while working, "I haven't met Patricia. Would you come and have dinner tomorrow?"

Jo replied, "Katharine, I haven't got the same energy that I had years ago when we worked together. After work, I like to be settled at home by eight o'clock!"

Her reply, "Oh, I hope so. I do hope so." A line from a play they had done years before.

One night we did have an early dinner with her, after which, she excused herself to go and wash her hair. She has become a real legend.

The marvelous actor Paul Scofield Jo had not met before, although we had seen his work. On *A Delicate Balance* they became good friends. They worked together very happily. Every time we went to England after that, our first evening out we would go and see Paul in his chosen play. I say "chosen play" because he is an actor whose life is the stage, and his home is the country in England.

* * *

After that, we went to Spain and we went to Italy, because Jo was offered a picture in both those countries.

Strangely enough, I knew Italy well and loved it. I loved it more each time I was there. However, although my father was Spanish and I had to speak Spanish to him all the time, my knowledge of Spain was practically nonexistent. I had made the picture with Orson Welles there, but we were working so hard I really never saw anything except the studio and my hotel. Of course, I had never seen so many nightdresses as I did in Spain, and the shops were lovely. Jo showed me around Madrid, and the Prado, which enchanted me, and we walked through the park together.

All the Latin languages are musical to me. My favorite (with apologies to my father) is Italian. But then, Daddy spoke and loved Italian, too. When we three girls had nurses or governesses, they were always Spanish. Daddy's English was quite poor. When I asked him why he hadn't studied English seriously, he replied, "What kind of an Englishman would I make?" But Mummy, the most English person I know, learned fluent Spanish! She had to cope with the staff and she intended to be understood!

Mummy had loved Seville when they went there (on their honeymoon), but she would have been happy to remain in England for the rest of her life. She almost did, except for occasionally visiting me in California and once in Italy.

Therefore, Jo and I introduced each other to Madrid. We took a large flat in a hotel. It had a kitchen, which was nice for making tea at odd hours, and, of course, as the Spanish have dinner around 11:00 P.M., the kitchen was there so we could have an early dinner while Jo was working. This turned out to be quite disastrous.

One evening, I tried to cook spaghetti for Jo. I boiled the pasta for 45 minutes and couldn't understand, when I went proudly to stir it, that it was a solid, almost immovable mass. Jo, of course, was gentle and kind to me. He tried to hide his laughter. The problem was solved when Orson told us about a little, marvelous French restaurant that served dinner at eight.

Nevertheless, we were both happy when the film finished and off we flew to Rome. No problem there with food. I spoke the language, which certainly helped Jo, and he enjoyed the picture. We visited all the places we loved. We had many friends — Americans and British — who had moved there to live.

We decided that as much as we loved it, we wanted to live in America but visit Italy often. At the time, we did not realize how very often that would be!

* * *

We both did a movie in Japan.

Our arrival in Tokyo was something we were not prepared for . . .

Stepping off the plane, we were greeted by five thousand camera bulbs flashing incessantly. We tried to push our way through the permanent wall of photographers, and were helped by several men and women whom we assumed to be with the film company.

They all carried immense bunches of flowers, and, without crushing these delicate, colorful blooms, ushered us into a tiny room inside the airport. *The Third Man* theme was playing loudly. As soon as we were seated, one after the other presented Jo with a bouquet. He was embarrassed, and, as he accepted them, he rapidly handed them to me!

An interpreter asked him unanswerable questions. She barely stopped between each query to give him time to answer, had he understood her.

I was sneezing into the garden that was covering me, while, at the same time, trying to help Jo by suggesting he could undergo this interview when we got to our hotel.

They took the flowers off me and handed them back to poor, bewildered Jo. Then they pummeled me with questions until I faked a fainting spell and we were helped into a motor car that took us to what was meant to be our hotel suite — but, we couldn't see any furnishings for it looked for all the world like a funeral parlor. I screamed. This time, it was not faked, but my allergy was, and it got us to another hotel where we found a lovely apartment with not a plant in sight.

They, by now, realized we were very tired and mercifully left us to rest in our new surroundings before we started working for them.

They were all charming and bowed constantly with no apparent reason, except, of course, that it was their custom. I considered the saying "when in Rome." Somehow, I didn't see how we could emulate the gracious Japanese and still do an American movie. It was a difficult picture, although the director was as helpful as he could possibly be. The title was *Latitude Zero*. It was science fiction and really none of us understood it too well. I would hazard a guess that the audience, when they saw it, was equally mystified!

Cesar Romero, a fine actor and a good friend, was in the film with us. He and I were the bad guys, which enabled us to occasionally get a few days off. Jo, being the hero, had to work incessantly and not under great conditions.

One day, Cesar said to me, "I'm tired of hotel food. I'd like to have some scrambled eggs and toast in your sitting room this evening."

"What a good idea," said I, not realizing what it would entail.

However, we went to the biggest department store and bought a one-ring burner and a pan. The plates and cutlery we thought we could get from room service. We had bought the utensils by just handing them to the man, then paying.

"Let's get the eggs," said Cesar, excitedly.

Down to the unbelievably vast food halls we went. After walking miles, lugging our small portable kitchen, we found the dairy products. The eggs were unreachable and crowded by other things, so we couldn't point to them.

A nice Japanese gentleman approached us and said something that we assumed was, "What can I do for you?"

Very slowly, in unison, and, almost in harmony, we said, *"We . . . would . . . like to buy some eggs."*

His inscrutable expression was not in the least encouraging.

We tried asking in Spanish, still harmonizing in unison. He shook his head without changing expression.

"Cesar, I think we should stop singing for our supper and take it in turns," I said.

I started very slowly in French. He waved his hand at me as if pleading me to stop.

"Oh, let's forget it," I said, almost in tears.

Cesar was not to be deterred. To my horror, he started quacking and clucking and mimed "laying eggs." The whole department stopped still and stared at us.

Then, the inscrutable became ingratiating. With a huge understanding smile, the man picked out a dozen eggs and handed them to Cesar, who gave him a handful of money, took my arm and led me out of the store amid much applause!

Except for the Kobe beef that we had sometimes in restaurants, those scrambled eggs were our best meal in Tokyo.

* * *

The work was exhausting, and Jo had been quite ill at the finish of the picture. He caught the Asian flu — in *Asia* — which, when he recovered, he described as his "elegantly timed weakness"!

Jo became extremely ill and, when I did finally get him to Honolulu, he remained in bed for three weeks in a hotel overlooking the ocean. I looked after him, as he didn't want nurses. He lived on lemonade and antibiotics. Then, when well enough, we went home.

I thought he would at least rest in between pictures, but my husband had unheard of recuperative powers. "Retirement" was a word he never used and was unable to accept.

* * *

We had gone to Russia where Jo performed in a film entitled *Joseph Cotten and the Performing Arts of Russia*. It had been freezing in Moscow and Leningrad and he had been doing night exteriors in a thin suit, as it was supposed to be springtime.

Our hotel was most unglamorous, but, our sitting room, although not very comfortable, had a fabulous position. It faced Red Square and the Kremlin, which would have been wondrous at any time, but, because this was the Fiftieth Anniversary of the Revolution, we were able to gaze at all the so-called leaders of the satellite countries assembling there. However we felt about it, we couldn't ignore its importance. The night lighting that glittered and gleamed and gave opulence to the famous square, the snow falling, even in daytime, it was a glorious sight, glorious but unreal.

I seldom went out. It was so painfully, unbelievably cold. That my husband was out there, in a spring suit, scared me. I worried about Jo.

He came back, his face was rigid and blue, but he was determined that we should go and watch Plisetskaya dancing in the then new ballet, *Anna Karenina.* Directed by her husband, Plisetskaya was no longer young but she was an *artiste par excellance.* Jo had to interview her for the film.

The theatre was the same temperature as it was outside. I insisted on wearing my coat round my shoulders, although it was against the rules. All coats should be handed to the lady in the cloakroom; Gentlemen went without coats.

I was adamant and said I would leave if I could not wear my coat. I won the argument, but . . . I worried about Jo.

* * *

We had been invited to dinner at the American Ambassador's private home. Ambassador Jacob Bean had twice been Ambassador to Russia with a spell in between. His wife was enchanting. She was a Californian and had a delightful sense of humor.

Jo wanted to know who had won the football game at home that day, and Ambassador Bean had his security men do whatever magic security men do and was able to tell Jo the winner! Fancy going to dinner in Russia at the American Ambassador's home and asking if he could find out the football score! Jo asked unabashedly and the Ambassador behaved as if this were a question he was asked every day.

I sat down and was confiding to Mrs. Bean some of the discomforts and peculiarities of the Russian hotels. She stopped me immediately, put her hands to her ears and pointed to the walls. I knew our room was bugged, and we were fairly careful, but this was the American Embassy.

"Here?" I asked in shock.

She shook her head in assent. I was floored. So, we changed the conversation immediately and I praised the ballet and the beauty of Leningrad. *Dr.* Murphy, the doctor in charge of the Embassy personnel, joined in our conversation. He was very nice. In fact, the evening was a joy, the most fun we had in the U.S.S.R.

* * *

The picture finished on New Year's Eve, and, although there was a party, we refused and went back to our hotel. We got into one single bed and tried desperately and unsuccessfully to keep each other warm. I had avoided the cold as much as possible, but . . . I worried about Jo.

* * *

The next morning, Jo was terribly flushed. I took his temperature. It was over 103 degrees. I called the American producer and said I needed him to see Jo as he was too ill to travel. He came immediately and realized the situation was serious.

"What can I do?" I asked desperately.

"We can only call a Russian doctor and they would immediately put him into a hospital here. That would worry me terribly. I'll go and speak to the assistant producer and see if he has any ideas. Jo can't travel home in that state."

He ran down the passage and left me alarmed as to what to do about my Jo, who looked at me through his feverish eyes and held my hand with his burning hands and said, "Don't worry, little thing. I'll just sleep and get better."

Of course, Jo would try that. He knew how upset I was. But, I knew he wouldn't get better by just sleeping.

I took a wild chance. I went to the phone and telephoned Mrs. Bean, the Ambassador's wife. I knew I wouldn't get her, but I could leave some sort of coded message. To my amazement, she came to the telephone right away and said, "We did have such an enjoyable evening. How nice of you to telephone."

I said in an over-calm voice, "My husband is a bit tired and is resting today. We met that charming *Mr.* Murphy at your lovely dinner party. (I was sure she understood that I was talking in code about *Dr.* Murphy.) He and my husband had so much in common and he said he had some good books that Jo would like. Do you think it would be possible for him to come over and visit with Jo for a little while? It would cheer him up so much."

Mrs. Bean was lightning quick in understanding my veiled, desperate call to see if Dr. Murphy could help Jo. "Funny you should mention that," she said. "He called this morning and said, 'Do you think it would be all right if I called Joseph Cotten — we really never finished our conversation on art?' I'll call him. I'm sure he'd love to visit your husband."

I quietly thanked her. We both knew our conversation was not private.

Dr. Murphy came to see Jo looking like a big fat man. Actually, he was slim, but he had a jacket and an overcoat filled with antibiotics and all the medications needed to cure Jo. He would have got into trouble if they had found out he was attending as a doctor; he was forbidden to medically treat any American visitors — just Embassy personnel. Within a few days, that wonderful man had Jo well enough to go to England and recuperate before leaving for the States a fit man.

We were never able to repay him for his desperately-needed attention. I also was unable to get in touch with Mrs. Bean to thank her. I have tried to find out where they were, as he retired just after we left. Sometimes ships that pass in the night drop their anchor round your heart. That was certainly so in this case.

* * *

Making the picture was most interesting. The crew and all the people we met were decent. It was just the wrong time of year.

* * *

We flew back to New York and checked into the Gotham Hotel to spend a few days there before going home to California. Only, it didn't turn out that way.

Waiting for Jo at the hotel was a script called *The Perfect Crime* to be made in Rome. It was such a good script that it would have been a perfect crime to turn it down. Of course, we returned to JFK Airport and took off for Rome. Valli, the lovely actress who had played opposite him in *The Third Man,* was also in the picture.

The *Perfect Crime* went very well in Rome, but we had to go to Vienna for four days' while shooting of the last few scenes. I had not expected such a big reception for Jo *there*, but, you see, thirty years earlier, when, of course, I was not married to him, he had made a really magnificent film in Vienna called *The Third Man.* They still had a picture of Jo and Orson by the ferris wheel. Of course, I had seen the picture, and I still remember that scene with the two of them on that great wheel.

One day when Jo was working, a gentleman telephoned me at the hotel, quite early in the morning. He introduced himself and said he had been an assistant on *The Third Man.*

I said, "I wasn't married to my husband then, so I'm afraid we do not know each other." He said he knew that, and that he was so glad that Jo had married me, and he was looking forward to our meeting. I told him we were only there for a short time and Jo would be working very hard, but, I said, if he could call him in the evening I was sure that Jo would remember him and look forward to a long chat.

"Mrs. Cotten," he said. "You, having seen that great movie, may remember that a large amount of it was shot in the sewers of Vienna." I laughed and said I certainly did remember, and that Jo had told me he was stunned by the cleanliness down there.

"That is one of the reasons that I'm telephoning you. Quite a few of the same sewer police who were in the picture with your husband and Mr. Welles are still there. They would like to invite you both to a party down there. I will speak to the producer of his present picture and see if he can give him an afternoon off. We would publicize his new movie, and, after the *Sewer Party,* Mr. Anton Karas (composer of *The Third Man* theme, on his zither) would like you both to go to his house and he will play you a little concert."

"That sounds absolutely marvelous. Please telephone my husband tonight. I'm sure he'd like to see all his friends again, and, if you can arrange it with his present producer, I know we'd love it."

He called Jo that night. Arrangements were made, and permission from the Italian producer, who was already thrilled at the amount of publicity Jo was getting in Vienna, said, "I am told by friends of mine who go to Vienna often that that picture is their pride and joy and is still running!!"

We went down to these pristine sewers. I had never been in a sewer before, so I did not have anything to compare them to, but you could have eaten off the floors. The Viennese were quite naturally very proud of them.

To see Jo being greeted by these men whom he had not seen for thirty years was most moving. They had brought bottles of wine, made sandwiches and we had a party. They called it a "welcome home" for Jo and begged him to make another picture there. I thought to myself, "If we get to New York and there's a script to be made in Austria, what, oh what would I do? Do I have to answer that?"

We then went to Mr. Anton Karas' home — another happy greeting. Mr. Karas sat at the piano and said he would play us some of his new compositions. I simply couldn't look at Jo, for Mr. Karas did not play the piano very well. He asked if he could change to his favorite instrument: the zither. Well, that was enjoyable, but, again, I kept from looking at Jo, for all his new compositions started quite lamely, and, seemingly unnoticed by him they all floated into *The Third Man* theme.

When we got back to the hotel, Jo said, "You know, darling — he is a very clever man . . . he became world renowned for composing one tune."

We have here, I feel, to give credit to that wondrous stubborn director — Sir Carol Reed. The studio wanted violins in Vienna; they wanted orchestras. Carol went out one night and heard this little man playing the zither. He insisted that was going to be the only instrument in the entire film. The heads of the studio fought him. He won.

Another thing for those of you who remember the picture, Valli walks past Jo at the end and never looks back — it is sad but right. Again, they fought him. The studio said, "Well, shoot another ending where she ends up with Jo." Carol said OK, but he didn't shoot it. He knew what would happen if he shot an alternate ending. He gave them the one he believed in, and he was right.

* * *

Upon completion of *The Perfect Crime* in Vienna, we finally went back to New York, at least to pick up the clothes we had left there when we departed so hurriedly.

I went to the beauty parlor near the hotel and left my Jo, hopefully, to have a nice long rest. Guess what? That work-aholic husband of mine didn't rest. Oh, no. He did something far more stimulating. He read a fascinating script that was to start immediately in Italy!

"But this is Venice, darling," he said, pleadingly. "Remember you said you were sorry we hadn't gone to Venice this time, you love it so. Of course, if you're tired, I can turn it down."

Apparently, it hadn't occurred to him that he was the one who should be (and probably was) tired.

"When do we leave?" I said, as calmly as I could.

"Tonight — eh, eh — the plane leaves at nine o'clock."

He looked like a little boy asking for a present. I couldn't resist that expression. I should have laughed, it was so ludicrous, but instead, I went to the telephone and called room service to cancel the bowl of Minestrone I had ordered for our supper.

It seemed to me it would be just enough to eat before settling down for an early night. What had made me choose minestrone, of all the soups on the menu!

Back to Italy we did go. This was a different Venice — we were not on the canal; we were in a magnificent mansion where the entire picture was shot. We lived on the premises. It was hugely comfortable. Jo and I had a lovely suite. The producers were man and wife. They were exceedingly charming but were really dilettantes; amateurs who probably would learn. They had a very good story called "Shadow on The Sun," but the plot (and it was a good plot) really relied on an experienced performance by a young boy. The boy they cast was quite beautiful and quite terrified! The poor child suffered each time the camera was on him, and it was on him a great deal. If he had had a touch of Freddie Bartholomew in him, it could have been not only an interesting, but very moving picture. It turned out to be just a "motion" picture. There was nothing moving about it. Jo played the young boy's father.

The Italians get very interesting stories, and, of course, they have many fine actors. The fine actors soon become stars, therefore, it's difficult to find just a good actor happy in a supporting part. I think the British handle casting most intelligently. Many "stars" think nothing of accepting a fairly small part and playing it superbly. There seems to be no "star system" in Britain. They are all actors and accept small and large parts with no class distinction.

Back to *Shadow on The Sun.* It was an enjoyable experience. The living was easy. We had marvelous meals in a lovely dining room, obviously prepared on the premises by an excellent chef. I would go for walks down the long driveway, crowded with trees and flowers, and immediately at the end was the main highway, no sidewalk. It was a perilous straight road into the Venice we had known: Gondolas on the canal; narrow cobble-stone streets; and, its own daring, glaring, almost-surrealistic light. Nothing, no way, no how, can compare with St. Mark's Square. I felt the same about it as I did on our honeymoon, and I will feel that way about it ad infinitum.

Suddenly, we both remembered that in six weeks' time, Jo was contracted to start work on a picture in Munich, for Bob Aldrich again, called *Twilight's Last Gleaming.* He was to start work on February 25th. This was about the fourth picture Jo would do directed by Bob. The last being the one in Mexico, *The Last Sunset,* with Kirk Douglas and Rock Hudson.

But on February 25th, he was still doing the last scenes on *Shadow on the Sun* in Venice. Bob said he could start February 26th — no later. They had to cancel our plane tickets to Munich, which were for February 26th, too late. The producer ordered a large car to drive us at midnight (when Jo had to finish his last shot) to Munich.

Also, we had to go over the Brenner Pass, as Innsbruck was six feet under snow. It was a long, dark, cold and perfectly beautiful drive. The Brenner Pass was kept clear by plows.

We opened our hamper, which contained sandwiches and champagne, and we drove through the Italian Alps, the Swiss Alps, the Austrian Alps and the Bavarian Alps.

On arriving at the Hilton Hotel in Munich, the porter said there was an important message for Jo.

It was a message from the Bavarian studios saying he was to be there at 8:00 A.M. It was now 7:00 A.M.! He had worked until midnight the day before and traveled all night, only to discover that he had time for a shower. He then went straight to work on another picture.

They broke for lunch and when they returned, they found Jo still on the set in his chair fast asleep. Dear Bob Aldrich used him in one more shot and sent him back to the hotel.

Jo was happy working with Bob again.

Somehow he found the strength to do the picture, then take me to England. There, I became painfully aware of how tired and completely knocked out my beloved husband looked. Finally, after a short stay, we were on our way home — to the States.

* * *

On the way back, I said, "Now, darling, I know you've worked very hard, but I have too. As soon as we get to New York, when we get to the hotel, anything to do with room service, anything to do with any orders, you are to do it. I'm tired of speaking Spanish, I'm tired of speaking Italian, and I'm tired of giving orders. You, my darling, are to answer the telephone, order anything. We are entering the United States of America and they can't understand my English accent."

Jo said, "I'll do it all, darling. So, relax."

We arrived at the St. Regis Hotel. We were sitting in the sitting room talking and the maid came in to turn down the beds.

"Jo, darling. Ask her for another two pillows," which he did.

Again, a little louder, thinking that she might be deaf. "Could we have another two pillows?"

"Eh?. . .eh?" was the reply. "*Non capisco, non parlo Inglese.*"

Jo came into me and shrugged his shoulders.

When he ordered dinner, the waiter was Mexican, his English was no better than the lady who'd done our room.

Jo said, "I think we'd better go home and then everyone will understand me."

Home we went, and what a joy it was to be together in our own surroundings.

* * *

Jo took up gardening again, and our terrace was blooming with glorious colors. I sat outside and painted. We both kept busy. If the telephone rang, anyone could answer it, or we'd just let the machine take messages.

For weeks we lazed. The working actors that we had become were now taking a civilized rest. Of course, we saw our friends. We had lunches on our terrace, particularly if people came from out of town.

I remember one terrace luncheon vividly, because it was so strange. John Gielgud, that famous British actor, was in Los Angeles working. One Sunday, we gave a moderately large lunch for him. The tables looked so pretty. In fact, I was proud of the whole place including the food. Naturally, I sat John on my right. I didn't know him awfully well, so I sat that marvelous Cathleen Nesbitt on his right. Aside from her talent as an actress, the great poet Rupert Brooke had been her lover until he died.

It was a highly-successful, pretty luncheon. Gielgud spoke mostly to Cathleen (They had been friends for years, that is why I seated them together). Also, he was a very shy man. They stayed quite late and all went home roughly at the same time.

Some weeks later, we were in England and we went to see John Gielgud in a play. He, of course, was excellent. We went back stage afterwards to congratulate him.

He was most gracious, slapped Jo on the back and said, "What a delightful time I had at your lovely Sunday lunch."

* * *

Then he turned to me and said, "I must compliment you on having such a beautiful place. I was so disappointed that you couldn't be there. You were away or something, weren't you?"

I am not often struck dumb.

I looked pleadingly at Jo for help. He just rolled his eyes and scratched his nose lightly, trying to hide his smile.

Now I had seated John on my right. I greeted him by saying, "I'm Patricia Cotten, you may not remember me. . ." (He'd only met me once.)

"Oh, yes, of course. I remember you. How lovely to see you again."

That was *then* —

It occurred to me to repeat the same conversation we'd had some months ago, but Ralph Richardson walked in with a large glass of whiskey, waved it in the air and said, "Cheers, everyone."

Then he looked at Gielgud and said evilly, "Have you had one already, Johnny boy?"

"I had no idea I was so easy to forget," I said, between laughter and tears.

"Just so he remembers his lines," said Jo, as he kissed me on the forehead.

* * *

Jo's good friend and director, Norman Foster, offered him a film in Utah. I believe it was based on a true story called *Brighty of the Grand Canyon*. The movie was entitled just *Brighty*. Jo was to play the owner of the little mule. Of course, he was called "Brighty" (not Jo, the mule).

We decided to drive to the Grand Canyon and break our journey at Las Vegas — one of Jo's least favorite places, except for the shows.

So, when we arrived there, we saw an early show and went straight to bed so we could complete our journey the next day.

* * *

Norman Foster was waiting outside the hotel. He rushed to meet us, grabbed hold of my arm and took me to the rim of the enormous, deep, unbelievable hole in the earth.

"Patricia," he said, "you are now seeing the eighth wonder of the world."

"Why don't they fill it in?" I said, thinking sensibly.

He was stunned for a while, and then he said, "You really are Spanish."

"Why, suddenly?"

"Well, when the first Spaniard was shown it, he said, *'No tiene ningun valor.'*"

I smiled, for that means, "It is of no use at all."

In different words, I said the same thing. Sometimes, my half-Spanish blood becomes fully *español*. Norman always thought I was more Spanish than English.

Jo and I settled into the hotel. I would go for long walks. The country was really beautiful. Jo worked very hard.

One day, he was not working. We were sitting in our hotel room. The telephone rang, Jo picked it up and went white.

"What is it?" I screamed. "You look in shock. What is it?"

Jo could hardly talk. "David," he whispered.

I started to cry. He didn't have to say anything else. I knew his dear friend, David Selznick, had died.

I rushed into Norman Foster's room, which was next door. He was standing stark naked. It didn't faze me. I was in shock.

"Norman, we have to go to Los Angeles. David Selznick is dead and we have to go and see Jennifer."

"I'll arrange it at once," said Norman.

I went back to our room. Jo was standing, still white and totally bewildered.

"What can I do?" he said.

"You do the most difficult — pick up the phone and call Jennifer. You won't get her, but leave a message that we'll be there tonight."

He telephoned Jennie and she came to the phone right away.

"Jo, what am I going to do?"

"We're coming right away," he said.

* * *

We got a helicopter as far as the Las Vegas Airport, then caught a plane to Los Angeles, and then drove a car up to the hills to try to give comfort and help to our very treasured friend.

As I recall, Jennie was in bed crying. It was awfully late.

Jo and David's sons, Geoffrey and Danny, discussed the arrangements for the funeral into the wee hours.

Poor Jennifer was bereft for quite a while over losing David. We saw her many times while she was grieving and lost.

In the garden of our Palm Springs house with one of his sculptures. He was proud of his work pants!

- 14 -

The Laughter Stops

One picture did come up for me which presented no apparent problem.

Robert Aldrich, our very good friend, and an equally good director, telephoned Jo. He said he was making a movie of the play *The Killing of Sister George* with actresses Beryl Reid, Susannah York and Coral Browne, and he wanted to know if Jo would be offended if he offered me a part of a prostitute! Two Southern gentlemen discussing a movie role!

"Would she have to undress?" asked my husband.

"No. Oh, absolutely not," answered the director, who was either protecting or insulting me.

"Then by all means, send the script, Bob." said the husband.

I read it and found the part quite a change and inoffensive, so I called Bob and accepted it.

"Oh, first, where are you shooting this?"

"Here and in England — you mostly shoot here and there's one silent shot in England that could be shot here on the back lot, but as you are Patricia Medina, how would you like to take your husband for a short trip to England? Work one day and then come home?"

The part began to assume marathon proportions. I told Jo. He loved the idea of getting a trip on his wife to our favorite city.

We decided to go to London ten days before they would be working there.

We arrived at our flat in the early morning after a very tiring flight from Los Angeles. Our little elevator took us straight into the entrance hall of our flat.

No sooner had we opened the door when Jo announced, "I am going to take a 24-hour nap, then I will show you all of London because you don't really know it as well as I do." (Actually, he was pretty correct.)

Off he went to take his nap. I, of course, called Piti and Gloria, and we all met for an early lunch and some shopping. We then went to see Mummy and Daddy.

Mummy immediately said, "Where's Jo?"

"Resting," I said.

"You look absolutely exhausted, darling. Why, when you've married such a marvelous man, can't you learn anything from him?

You should have gone straight to bed so that tomorrow you would be ready to enjoy being here."

"I thought you'd like to see me," I said, in a hurt tone.

"Of course I like to see you. We all are overjoyed at seeing you, even if you're dead tired. You may be the happiest married woman in the world but you are still my daughter. Now go home and go to bed like a good girl."

I did as I was told.

I walked into the flat quietly, so as not to disturb Jo. But, there he was, in the drawing room, in a lovely silk robe.

"I thought you were having your nap?"

"I had almost six hours sleep. I knew your mother would send you to bed, so I woke up and made you some tea, then we can go back to bed together and be ready for tomorrow."

"What happens tomorrow?"

"Well, my darling actress wife brought me over on this trip. I'm not very good at being a kept husband, so I called Claridges and booked a table for lunch tomorrow. I am giving a luncheon party. I telephoned Piti when you were on your way back here and told her to ask them all to meet us there at a quarter to one. Come darling, it's getting late and the bed's getting cold."

Again, I did as I was told.

* * *

Walking into the lounge at Claridges Hotel, the violins were playing soft old tunes. Jo said, "I'm glad no one's told them that World War I is over!"

The somellier came up to us as the others started arriving.

"The same as usual, Sir?" he said to Jo.

Jo hadn't been there for several years but he treated us as if we had been in yesterday.

When we all went into lunch, I noticed that every table had flowers except ours. I was a bit jealous until the head waiter walked up and put a beautiful arrangement on our table. The flowers were exactly the colors that I was wearing and, of course, different from all the other tables. Without ordering, we were brought the same wine we'd had when we were last in London.

When we finished our main course, the waiter said, "Your creme brulée will be ready in a minute." We were all most impressed.

Jo said, "This is the way a hotel should be run, and this is why we will always come here."

We went to the theatre and we saw a naughty English comedy called *No Sex Please, We're British*. We also went to Covent Garden and heard *Madame Butterfly*. Puccini always tears my heart out.

When we were in Italy, Jo had taken me to see Puccini's little house. The piano was there and an incomplete start of an opera. Outside, they had built a statue of him. It seemed, from the pictures we'd seen, to be a perfect likeness. Inside his lips, had been carved the ever-present cigarette.

Puccini died too early. If he had known what we know today, would he have stopped smoking? I do not know. It is not often that I am that indefinite, but, about such monumental talent I have no knowledge, nor would I hazard a guess about its weaknesses.

We had dinner quietly at home.

We ran into Shirley MacLaine on Bond Street. She was from Virginia also so she and Jo had an understanding. Just a "hello, how are you?" They respected each other's privacy.

After a while, it was getting close to the time that I would be hearing from the *Sister George* company. We had two more days before they descended upon us.

We stayed home and did crossword puzzles. We watched British TV. We saw other friends. Then I was called to work the following morning, but it was cancelled because it rained.

Everyone stayed in. The following day, the rain was heavier and the weather forecast was dire.

It rained nonstop for three straight weeks. That wouldn't have been so terrible, except Jo was due back the following day to start a television film. He had signed the contract.

I took him to the rainy airport and held him, my tears mixing with the rain. "We've never been separated," I cried.

"I'll telephone as soon as I get home." He was gone.

He telephoned me at some ungodly hour. "When are you coming home?"

"It's stopped raining. I'll take my suitcase to the set."

When I got to the set, Bob said, "Get out of that taxi and walk into the white mew's house."

I did exactly that.

"Now, get the hell out of here and take the same taxi to the airport, you'll just make the plane."

You bet I did!

* * *

Los Angeles:

The door opened, I was the first out and in his arms. We stood entwined for a long time.

In all the years that we have been married, we were separated for one day. It was hell.

* * *

When Bob and the rest of the company returned from England, we continued the picture in Bob's studio.

The Killing of Sister George had been a great success as a play in England, and I believe New York.

The story was rather sad — a mixture of comedy and tragedy, actually.

Beryl and Susannah are lesbians in love and happy. Beryl played Sister George, a television character, much loved by audiences.

Coral Browne played the head of the television station. She was also a lesbian.

Come to think of it, I was the only "straight man" in the film!

I had a marvelous comedy scene at the end which was "cut out" because someone had the bright idea that Coral should finally make love to Susannah, and Beryl comes in just in time to watch the climax.

The shock value was supposed to cause a sensation, and make a fortune for the film. I didn't see the scene but I find it very easy to believe that instead of an exciting shock, it was criticized for being handled in poor taste.

In the play, the relationship came across without even any kissing. It was a love story about two people whose sexual preference, though different from the majority, was woven into the story delicately and clearly. The scene that Coral agreed to do (against her will) with Susannah (who kept running off the set crying before finally settling into it) hit the lesbianism with a sledge hammer, and the love became a doubtful emotion.

I know, of course, that I must have had a slight chip on my shoulder because I lost my funny scene. But my true belief is that through this Beryl lost her chance at being nominated for an Academy Award. She gave a wonderful, funny and very touching performance that became overshadowed.

After the film, we gave a luncheon party for all the actors and the director Bob and his wife, Sybil. Beryl arrived in what I can only describe as a very flimsy slip, almost "see through," with little spaghetti straps that kept slipping down, and she was most generously endowed!

She had never met Jo, but as soon as she caught sight of him, she tore across the room, flung her arms around him and said, "Oh, you beautiful creature. I've always adored you. I hope you don't mind?"

My conservative, Southern husband looked down at this ample, half-dressed woman and asked with a little smile, "Is it all right if I call you Beryl?"

She tugged at one of her spaghetti straps that seemed to be giving way and said, "What had you planned to call me, Steve?"

"Yes," he replied. "Come on, Steve. Let's get a drink."

They became instant friends. We had a fun lunch — and Beryl, who is a gourmet cook, invited us to several dinners.

* * *

Don Taylor and his wife, Hazel Court, had been neighbors of ours in the Palisades, as well as very good friends. Don was a very good actor — a handsome leading man. Hazel, at that time, was still a beautiful leading lady. They both changed their careers. Don became an excellent director, and Hazel is now a highly-successful sculptor. She goes every year to Italy to buy Carrara marble to work with.

Some time ago, Don was going to make a picture in Munich called *Jack of Diamonds*. He offered Jo a good part in it which he accepted. We decided to stop in London for a week before going to Munich.

I was talking to my sister Gloria on the telephone. She and Gerry now lived in Beaconsfield, Hertfordshire. After Gerry left the Air Force, he worked for British Petroleum. Gloria told me he had to leave on business for about three weeks.

"Oh, how wonderful," said I.

"I don't think it's at all wonderful," replied a sorrowful Gloria.

"What I mean is that it's wonderful for me. Would you come with me to Munich, and while Jo works, we can be together and get to know the city?"

"When do we leave?" was the more cheerful reply from Beaconsfield.

"On Tuesday."

"That's the same day Gerry goes away."

We made our plans. We could, all three of us, leave together. When I told Jo, he was delighted.

"Oh, darling, I'm so happy for you. You and Gloria always laugh so much together. I hate to think of you alone in a foreign country while I work."

We flew to Munich. Jo and I had a lovely corner suite at the Four Seasons Hotel. We managed to get another room for Gloria, adjoining our sitting room.

Now, although I am considered somewhat of a linguist, German is not one of my languages.

Jo went off to work. Gloria and I spent a lot of time in the sitting room ordering room service. You see, the hotel staff spoke English!

* * *

One day the heating went off. We were freezing. I asked the waiter who had brought in our breakfast to send a plumber. He clicked his heels and said he would.

After a while, a fat red-faced man came in and said something quite unintelligible.

Gloria sat on the sofa and tried to hide her giggles.

I was not to be deterred.

"It . . . is . . . *cold . . . we — need . . . heat.*"

He looked at me as if I had just told him the joke of the century. He laughed so loudly his stomach shook.

"Yah — yah, yah."

More laughter and by now Glory had to try a more obvious approach.

She pointed to the radiator and started shivering.

More laughter.

I got one of the blankets from the bedroom and put it round me. Finally, I lay on the floor shivering, sneezing and coughing.

"*Cald,*" I yelled.

"Yah, yah, yah!"

Glory said, "Stop it, Pat. Whatever will he think of you?"

"He doesn't know I'm an actress," I said indignantly.

"He does now," said Glory between the seemingly incessant "Yah, yah, yah."

In desperation I said, *"Il fait froid, pourquoi ce n'est pas possible — sneeze — d'arranger le chauffage?"* (It is cold, why isn't it possible — sneeze — to arrange the heating?)

I had just about started to cry when "Ludwig of Bavaria" said softly, *"Madame, vous avez froid?"* (Madam, are you cold?)

"Oui, j'ai froid, mais je pense que c'est impossible que vous pouvez m'arranger la chauffage?" (Yes, I'm cold, but I think it's impossible for you to give us heating.)

"Oui, oui. C'est absolument possible." (Yes, yes. It's absolutely possible.)

His *"oui's"* were more secure than his *"yah's."*

Within minutes after he'd kissed my tiny frozen hand, we were *boiling.*

I told Gloria that we really had to get out of the hotel. Even if we had to fight the language, *so be it.* We put our heaviest coats on, rushed out from the heat and walked for miles in the cold.

I saw a little, typically German restaurant and announced, "this is where we will have lunch!"

It was fairly crowded, and at least it was warm. We found a nice little table almost in the middle of the room which was rather more conspicuous than we wanted. It seemed the only empty one, so we took it.

An extremely businesslike waitress marched up to us bearing the largest, longest menu I have ever seen.

She thrust one into each of our hands and stood at attention. Finally she spoke.

"Was wollen sie trinken?"

Gloria eyed me with enormous questioning eyes above the huge menu.

"Trinken . . . eh, drink," I snapped at her.

She smiled at the waitress and said, *"Ein Bier."*

I tried to look as dignified as possible and said, *"Wasser — minerale?"*

"Focking is gut," she said.

"I know it is but I want a drink."

"Oh - eh. Yah!"

Gloria had slipped silently under the table. Her menu cluttered to the floor.

The waitress disappeared as if by magic and reappeared the same way, bearing a glass tankard with at least two gallons of beer which she dumped in front of Gloria's empty place. Then with a complete change of personality, she delicately, almost reverently, placed a large bottle of F——ing water in front of me.

I moved her away, pointing to my menu, giving the impression, I hoped, that we would order later.

I had to use all my strength to get Glory under control and also to behave myself. I could feel hysteria approaching rapidly.

"Get up at once and pull yourself together. You're a spectacle."

Her reappearance was not silent. She couldn't get up completely without leaning all over the table and upsetting our unfortunate drinks. Her face appeared, huge mascara tears streaming onto the pristine white tablecloth. I got up and went to help her. She was shaking like jelly.

"Everybody's looking at us, please stop."

She stopped at once, looked at me seriously and said, "It's all your fault. Why do you always have to be different? You could have had a beer. But no, you had to go and order your F——! Water."

We both exploded into loud and vulgar laughter.

A gentleman at the table behind us looked at Glory and said, "Vas a gut one, no?"

Glory said, "Yah, a very gut vun — "

He joined in with our laughter, then lent her an extra napkin to finish wiping her "tear-stained" half-black face.

Eventually, we quietly resumed our seating and studied helplessly the huge incomprehensible menus. At least they hid our faces — and most of our bodies.

Finally, I dared to speak. "Darling, you said you learned some German in school. Don't you understand anything?" I waited, not daring to say another word in case the dam burst again.

A very subdued Gloria lowered her menu, looked at me as if her German was flawless and said proudly, "If you will look at one hundred and ninety-two (I think) on this placard, you will see that it says very clearly in English *Irish Stew*."

Well, that set me off. I checked the menu and wiping my eyes, I read *Irish Stew*.

Brunhilde reappeared.

Gloria looked her straight in the eye and said, "Zwei Irish Stew."

Then I burst out laughing. The Irish stew was a plate of boiling garbage. Try as we did, we could not eat it.

Glory drank a gallon of beer. I couldn't take the top off my bottle — Glory's gentleman friend came and removed it for me and poured me a glass.

The bill came. In my shame, I left her the biggest tip in the world.

When Jo got back from work, he said he could hear us laughing from the elevator!

* * *

After our experience in the typical little German restaurant, we decided to change our tactics. We did go out to lunch every day, *but* we went to well-known places where they were used to tourists and we could speak English. We never ordered water. There was a lot delivered to our hotel suite bearing the outrageous name.

The Bavarians are very nice people.

The movie was happy for Jo. I was sad when I had to take Gloria to the airport to return home to Gerry. We did agree that any time Jo had to work in Europe, and Gerry was away on business, Glory would be with me.

* * *

Some time later, we went to Rome.

Jo and I adored Rome, and we were there often.

The da Vinci Airport we had begun to know. Then the drive (perilous though it may have been) passing all the full Italian cypress — until the traffic drivers screamed to each other and drove all over the Roman streets with no respect for pedestrians or buildings. Up the Via Sistina and with a screeching happy halt, we were deposited at the Hotel de Ville.

We were picking up Mummy and Daddy the next day, so we hired a car and a very careful driver, Guiseppe, who drove them slowly and gently to the hotel.

We had taken the penthouse there that Paulette Goddard and her husband Erich Maria Remarque used very often. The elevator came straight up to the apartment which was not really large, but it had the most enormous terrace I have ever seen — with a view of St. Peter's and almost all the rest of Rome. It was peaceful, it was beautiful, it was in fact without apology, "heavenly."

Daddy was so happy in Rome. He had spent much of his youth there. After leaving the University of Seville, he went to Rome, just travelling, and he learned to speak fluent Italian. I also learned to speak fluent Italian (though not at the same time, obviously!). Daddy still had quite a few friends there. Mummy and I would walk down the Via Sistina looking at the shops.

One day, we stopped at a beauty parlor. We saw glamorous wigs in the window and then and there both decided to become blondes.

I let them cut all my hair off first, so it would be quicker. Then they bleached a short snappy platinum blonde.

When Mummy saw mine she decided to take a chance, but she decided not to go quite as curly and blonde as I.

She was sitting sleepily under the hair dryer, when a rather reticent English woman came in. She couldn't make herself understood by the hairdresser, so I translated for her. She was delighted to know that I was English too!

At that moment, Mummy, still under the dryer, lifted it and took a peek.

She dropped the hair dryer back with a thud (so she couldn't hear a thing). "Patricia, get me some gin," she yelled in a panic.

I went over, lifted up the hair dryer and said clearly into her ear, "There's an English lady sitting there and she can hear you."

"I don't care who's there, bring me some gin at once. Daddy will divorce me, and you look like someone else's daughter. Hurry up!"

I dashed out and bought a tiny bottle of gin which she drank in one gulp.

Actually, when she was dry, she looked very nice indeed.

* * *

We got back to the hotel and waited for Daddy. He walked in, slowly took off his hat, hung up his walking stick and sat down.

"Do either of you two ladies know how I can get some coffee?" he said nicely.

We didn't answer.

Mummy walked out of the room and I said, "Don't you think she looks nice?"

"Very nice," he said, "but, who is she?"

I ordered him some coffee and went into the other room, where Mummy and I both fiddled with our hair.

When Jo got back from work we were all silently sitting in the sitting room.

To my mother he said, "Hello, Gonda, as he gave her a kiss.

"You do look nice."

He then came over and kissed me.

All evening he behaved as if nothing had happened.

Just before we went to sleep, with his back to me he said quietly, "You always look beautiful my darling, but maybe one day you'll look just like the girl I married."

My roots began to sting, then my eyes began to sting. He had not made love to me.

Next morning, Mummy and I went back to the "Chamber of Horrors."

We had suffered to be glamorous and different. Now we sat quietly through all the pain that would make us our ordinary, natural, and hopefully, loved selves.

That evening, neither of our husbands remarked about our sacrifice. At least they pretended not to notice.

We said "good-night" to the "old folk."

Jo lifted me in his arms and carried me to bed . . . kissing my dark curls as he walked. He lay me gently on the bed and sat down beside me and started to undo the buttons of my blouse.

"Why do you have such complicated button holes?"

"To make it difficult for you to undo them!"

"Patricia, what have I done to make you unhappy?"

"Nothing tonight. Actually, you're being very nice."

He had completed the difficult task of undoing my blouse, and was now pulling my skirt off with comparative ease.

He gave me a wide-eyed, innocent stare and said, "When have I not been nice to you?"

"Last night, you were cold and horrid."

"Last night, a blonde woman got into bed with me. I had been expecting my 'Spanish Beauty.' Isn't that how Bob Aldrich refers to you?"

"I am not married to Bob Aldrich."

"And a very good thing, too. Anyway, I don't recall doing anything last night to upset you" —

I took a long pause, for by now, I was completely undressed and I was finding it difficult to be dignified.

I turned my face away from him and said, softly and boldly, "It's what you didn't do that upset me."

He moved away. I thought he was going to walk out of the room. Suddenly, he came back, pulled the covers over me and got in beside me.

I started to cry softly. We so seldom had any disagreements. He had spoiled me constantly since our marriage and I wanted it to go on.

He took me in his arms and kissed my tears. I was so relieved. I clung to him, fearing that he might turn his back.

"Darling, you'll have to allow me overtime. You see, I've needed you so terribly since yesterday evening."

I tried to whisper to him, but he sealed my lips with a kiss. It was so complete, so wondrous that it seemed kissing was invented just for us.

Oh, yes indeed . . . it was.

* * *

Germany seems to have played a larger part in our travels than I had realized: In Munich, the movie for Don Taylor, where Gloria and I behaved so badly; the few days when Jo finished the Italian picture in Vienna; and again, in Munich, for Bob Aldrich's movie after Jo had worked so hard in that castle in Venice.

Now, I remember a very happy time in the beautiful city of Hamburg — Jo had written a charming book entitled *Vanity Will Get You Somewhere* (his autobiography), and we had traveled a lot with it.

In Hamburg, a young and efficient man handled the book signing and our stay there. His name was Gerhardt Schwartz. He signed his books all over the U.S., and in England, and so it was a joy to him that Mr. Schwartz made everything easy and enjoyable. There was a delightful party for us with entertainment. He took us round the immaculate city and then out into the country. It was different, so efficient was everything that we were asked to do.

A television reporter wanted to talk with Jo and he was very tired and weak. He begged off, as he felt he would not be his most eloquent, but the lady came back and said, "I don't want you to say a word."

Jo looked stunned. She laughed at his expression and said, "In your book, you mention that you make the best martinis in the world, or something slightly more modest! Anyway, I have all the ingredients that you said you used, so I thought I would say, 'Mr. Cotten, would you be so kind as to make me one of your famous martinis? I have everything here for you.' Then you, being the gentleman that you are, will make me a martini (in silence) and hand it to me, and I will give you my verdict!'"

Jo made her martini with a flourish here and there and handed it to her with a daring look which did not seem to faze her. She took one sip, looked heavenward and said, "Perfect." Jo bowed to her and she went on sipping. End of show. It was seen all over Germany and was a huge success. (So few people who have TV shows have the imagination to think up something as ingenious and different and really amusing.)

When we saw this brilliant television reporter later she appeared a little glassy-eyed but sober. I had great admiration for her and heaved a sigh of such relief. Jo's martinis, I'm told, (I never dared taste one) are the best — and almost lethal!

* * *

We decided to stop in England to see the family and rest a bit before going home.

I have to mention Orson again. We had many weekends at his house in Spain. It seemed we were like family. We met his wife, Paola, and his young daughter, Beatrice, who is still a very good friend. He never repeated or referred to his telling me that his "best friend" was the only person who could cope with me.

The first time we saw him after our marriage, he embraced and congratulated Jo, then he gave me a long penetrating look. Half smiling, he kept on looking until I had to turn away. It was the one and only time in my life I felt I was blushing!

a

a) With Jimmy Stewart and his Gloria at Jo's first book signing, which they hosted.
b) A compliment from famed author Sidney Sheldon. Jo was surprised.

b

Of course, he and Jo had worked together in the Mercury Theatre and had become instant friends.

They are completely different personalities. Perhaps, that is why their performances on the screen complimented each other (i.e., *Citizen Kane, The Third Man,* and *Journey into Fear.*)

Orson is the most eloquent person I have ever met.

Once when we were visiting Piti and Ken in Cadogan Square London, Orson phoned and said he was on the other side of the square, which immediately garnered him an invitation to come over for a drink.

"It's dark. How will I find the house?" said the spoiled genius.

Orson and Jo, two brilliant actor friends.

"I'll meet you in the middle of the square and I'll wear my *Third Man* coat," was Jo's reply.

"I'm leaving now," stated Orson.

My nephew Christopher was in bed with a slight cold.

"Who was on the phone?" he called out.

"Orson Welles. He's on his way over," replied his mother.

Within an instant, Christopher appeared in the drawing room. His cold left him as the doorbell rang.

Piti and Ken have some beautiful furniture; one piece is a wonderful, long delicate bench by William Kent. No one is ever allowed to sit on it even for an instant.

The two actors came in; Jo stood by the fire, Orson sat on the William Kent. Drinks were offered. As the bench creaked, Orson ordered a brandy.

Christopher asked him a million questions. I wish I had a recording of the glorious, edifying answers.

Two hours and a bottle of brandy later, he stood up to take his leave . . . obviously, out of pride or respect for such a brilliant weight, the William Kent made not a sound. We watched from the balcony as he walked back across the square.

"Wasn't he splendid?" said Christopher.

"He certainly was," we replied, as the empty bottle of brandy was discarded.

* * *

Jo and I returned to our flat, sat by the Adam's fireplace and wondered after leaving the following week, when we would return to its warmth.

Jo was very tired after working so consistently while at the same time entertaining my family and keeping me blissfully happy. He fell asleep on the sofa by the fire. His hand was holding mine. I dared not move for fear of disturbing his much-needed rest.

I turned to Jo. He was still holding my hand, his eyes were closed, and his breathing was so light I could hardly hear it. He opened his eyes.

"Oh, darling. I'm so sorry. I fell asleep."

"You are very tired. I think we should go home a little sooner . . . say, in a couple of days' time. Then you can rest for at least a month without taking a trip — not even to San Francisco. Perhaps you should go and have Dr. Forde look you over."

"I don't think there's anything wrong with me. Would you like to go out to dinner?"

"No, darling," I replied. "Norah left us a casserole. All I have to do is heat it up. I'd much rather stay in. Do you mind?"

I went into the kitchen, heated up the dinner and got it all ready. I walked back into the room with a small glass of white wine for each of us.

He was asleep again.

As he lay there sleeping, I noticed how pale he was. He usually had a marvelous color.

Sensing my presence in the room, he opened his eyes.

"Jo, you have every reason to be thoroughly exhausted. I don't think you realize how you have never stopped working since we got married."

No reply.

We ate dinner quietly. Jo didn't eat much. The fire still crackling, he lay back on the sofa, closed his weary eyes and dozed off once again.

I thought to myself, "Yes, as soon as we get home I'll call Dr. Douglas Forde, his fine physician. He can check his heart and his lungs. I have complete confidence he will look after Jo as no one else can."

* * *

The next morning, I called the family and T.W.A. and all arrangements were made for an earlier departure home, no stop in New York, no offer that Jo couldn't refuse.

Straight home and a thorough check-up . . .

a) *The dress I wore to Bette Davis' dinner.*
b) *Rehearsing*
c) *Douglas Fairbanks Jr.*
d) *With Sexy Rexy in* Foxes of Harrow
e) *With Fernando Lamas & Arlene Dahl*
f) *With Dennis O'Keefe*
g) *On the way back from England, Mummy made me take the ship.*
h) *Covered up from head to foot (nice change)*

a) With Alan Ladd in England
b) On location, I think I'd been shot.
c) Fred Astaire
d) In Richmond, Virginia, with the governor and his wife
e) Jennie was always pretty
f) With my literary agent, Dorris Halsey
g) Rehearsing bath scene—cameraman only allowed in, but I was dressed.

a) *Flirting with Paul Henried*
b) *Always a "bad girl"*
c) *First "good girl" roll*
d) *Co-starring with MacDonald Carey in* Stranger at my Door
e) *Really bad girl!*
f) *First still taken before I became an actress. I had to borrow the a dress from the photographer's wife.*
g) *Receiving an award in Barcelona*
h) *Bob & Dolores Hope*

BOOK TWO

Only When I Cry

Always together.

- 15 -

The Pain Begins

When we got home, Jo had a bad cold and was made to stay in bed for a few days. I left to wash my hair, for I was going out to lunch.

When I returned to our bedroom, Jo was in his bathroom. I could hear the shower running, running, running. It seemed to me that he was staying there too long, especially as he still had a cold. I never would enter his bathroom, but I did go into his dressing room and as I went in, I heard him call, "Patricia."

I flew to the bathroom door, opened it and Jo came staggering out. His knees were red. He had fallen in the shower. Now he was reeling in his dressing room.

I grabbed him and called out for our housekeeper, Shirley. She came at once.

"Hold him," I yelled, "while I call Dr. Forde."

Dr. Forde told me to hang up and call the paramedics immediately, which I did.

Shirley, God bless her, was strong and aware that something awful had happened. She held this naked man, got him to sit down, and she put his pajamas on him and slowly walked him back to bed. All the time he kept saying, "I'm all right. I'm all right."

I tried to soothe him and wondered how long the paramedics would take to arrive. I have no criticism of this group as a whole, but Shirley and I thought they were too long in coming.

They asked me a lot of questions, put Jo on a stretcher and gave him a shot. Douglas Forde telephoned to see what was going on, he asked to speak to one of the paramedics, after which he spoke to me.

"He's had a stroke, Patricia. They're taking him to Cedars Sinai. Get in the ambulance with him and I'll see you there. Cedars is your nearest hospital." I remember the date. It was June 8, 1981. *age 76*

I knew that we had desperately needed Douglas Forde. He had been our physician for many years, and Jo had always had such faith in him.

I got in the front seat with the driver while Jo lay in the back being tended to. I wondered why they didn't use the siren to go to the hospital. Here was a desperately-ill man in need of attention and we seemed to be going at a snail's pace. Of course, there are reasons for everything, and at that time my reasoning seemed nonexistent. I was at a point of hysteria.

They took him away from me in the hospital and told me to wait. That is when moments seem like hours and hours seem like years.

A couple was walking past me and the gentleman came over to sit beside me on the sofa.

"Don't sit down now, Jack. We've seen Ellen and she's doing fine. Let's go," said the wife.

"I've just heard they've brought a movie star in here and he's not expected to live. I want to find out who he is," said the husband as he seated himself beside me.

I got up and walked away.

* * *

As I was standing, praying quietly, Dr. Forde came up behind me and said, "Where is he?"

"They took him into a little room somewhere down there. I was allowed in for a minute."

Douglas ran toward the little room and was gone. When he finally returned, he sat me down and said quietly, "Patricia, you'll have to go home and wait. I'll keep in touch with you."

"But I must speak with him," I cried.

"He cannot speak," was the awful reply.

"But when I went in to see him he said, 'Hello, little thing.'" (He always called me that.)

Douglas seemed surprised and doubtful. "Are you sure he spoke?"

"Absolutely," I was now crying.

"Let's see if we can go back and take a look at him," he said.

We went in. My beloved husband was lying with tubes and bottles sticking into his arms. There was a big plaster on the back of his neck.

He looked at me silently and painfully. I was afraid to touch him so I leaned over and said, "Do you know my name?"

He shook his head very slightly, it meant no.

"I'm your wife," I said.

He moved his head the other way and tried to smile. That meant yes.

Well, he knew I was his wife and for the time being that was all that mattered.

The neurologist walked in and asked me to leave.

"When will he speak again?" I pleaded.

"His speech may return in eight hours. If not, I'm afraid he won't speak again."

He almost pushed me out of the room and I disliked him. Thank God Dr. Forde was there.

Going back home was awful. Everything in the apartment reminded me of him. I looked at the terrace, at his flowers and his trees, and as I walked out there I could hear his voice. That voice.

How could God silence that voice forever? He wouldn't; he couldn't. I looked up at the sky and felt that somehow we would be helped. I walked inside again. Whatever the result of this massive stroke, I had to have him back. In the final analysis, that was really all that mattered. Together we could accomplish anything.

They had said eight hours. Oh, what a long time eight hours is.

At the dreaded hour, I returned to the hospital. Jo was silent. The patch on his neck, I discovered, was a temporary "Pacemaker." His heart required a pacemaker, but as they had given him Coumadin to thin his blood, he couldn't have a permanent one yet.

The neurologist came in and told me that Jo would never speak again. He had lost his speech entirely.

"I will not accept that diagnosis," I said. "He will speak again no matter what you say."

"Then he'll have to start again like a child, from A B C."

"So be it," I said and turned away from him.

I sat quietly beside Jo until the neurologist left. Some time later, two very nice nurses came in and asked me to leave as they had to attend to him.

* * *

Gloria and Piti had called non-stop from England, and finally, against my insincere argument, Piti told me that she and Ken were arriving the following day.

How typical that she had not hesitated when she heard of our plight, and immediately they were coming 6,000 miles on a flight of mercy.

I have become very Americanized since living here, and much more so since marrying an American, but as I lay in bed that night, I felt proud of my British upbringing. The British never flag nor falter in times of stress. Through my half-closed eyes, I dimly saw the Union Jack approaching the Statue of Liberty. I don't believe I slept, but during the night came the full impact of what had happened to Jo.

* * *

When Jo moved to a private room, accompanied by all his machinery, I was there all the time and he was smiling. Several times Piti and Ken were allowed to see him and gave him words of comfort.

There was so much he was trying to say. His brain was clear but the words just wouldn't form.

Douglas Forde came from Malibu constantly to check on him, and his soothing presence helped Jo enormously.

For two weeks he lay in bed. He was speechless and just occasionally smiled when I held his hand and stroked his head. He understood what I said but he was not able to utter a sound. Still, in my mind, I could hear that wonderful voice of his, that unique voice.

He was determined, when he was well enough, to start lessons, and before he left the hospital, he did start. A fine little speech therapist named Susie came to help him. But he was too weak, and after a quarter of an hour, he fainted. He had started too soon.

I decided to tell a few friends about his stroke, but I never used the word "massive" as it had been described to me.

I told Jo's two nephews, Sam and Joe, and his brothers who phoned regularly, and I tried to minimize the whole thing and comfort them. I thought that if Whit flew in from Virginia, or Sam from Boston, Jo might think I'd sent for them and suspect the worst.

At last, they told me he could return home the following morning! He was thrilled and terrified, as indeed was I. He had only walked the passage once and his legs were like rubber.

Dr. Forde and I removed him from his room. I fetched the car, and Dr. Forde practically lifted him in beside me.

The buildings and the traffic scared him. I wondered if he knew how scared I was? I will never know how I got him through the large lobby of our apartment building. Although he had lost a great deal of weight, he was still a big man for anyone (particularly not a very large woman) to almost carry.

Worse was to follow. He did not recognize the apartment. The place was almost entirely mirrored. I had it done that way to reflect our collection of Comedia dell'arte. But now I could see that he was bewildered by the reflections, and he was growing weaker by the minute. Shirley and I put him to bed where he fell asleep immediately for quite a long time.

When he awoke, I was sitting beside him and I could see he recognized our room. *Our* room. He patted the bed and waved his arms around, pointing at pictures on the wall, smiling.

Oh, what a joy to have him home and an even greater joy to see his brain was undamaged.

Shirley made him a malted milk which, much to her delight, he devoured.

- 16 -
A - B - C

And so began an interminable recuperation period. One thing was clear to us both; there is no such thing as "giving in." Though your heart may sob, though you feel it is all dreadfully unfair, though you want to wallow in tears, tears that you hope might wash the whole nightmare away, it doesn't happen that way. Determination, positive thinking, and *work, work, work* had to be his everyday routine.

Jo started work again with Susie. She was very patient, but Jo wanted to do too much, so Susie would say, "that's enough for today," and home we went.

Pretty soon he was doing an hour a day of therapy. We would drive to the hospital at 1:00 P.M. and return home at 2 P.M.

The first word he said was, "Zung." Not very encouraging, but so welcome.

Then one day he said, "Thank you."

I looked at him ecstatically as though he had recited Hamlet from beginning to end.

"That's very clever," I said. "I'm glad you're going to be polite, it will make it much easier to nurse you."

One hour every day of work. Trying to say "cat" or "dog" or any three-letter words. I was beginning to wonder what he would do when it came time to say four-letter words. Perhaps he would be able to write a book consisting entirely of four-letter words, and maybe have a best seller!

He picked up the playing cards and started playing Solitaire. I watched once and realized that he was playing perfectly. I don't know why he had no trouble at all with the cards, but it was a wonderful step forward; a great deal of time sped fast while he proudly and constantly played Solitaire. That lonely game became his best friend. You see, he was unable to read, and he still couldn't say my name.

* * *

One night, there was a beautiful harvest moon. Jo was on the terrace and he called me to come and look at it. I flew to the terrace, tears streaming down my face, as he held me close and said, "What's . . . matt. . .?"

"You called me 'Patricia,'" I said.

How or where it came from, he was unaware of, but unfortunately, he did not call me that again for some time.

* * *

When we were driving home from his weekly check-up, a little sports car drove through a red light and nearly crashed into our car. Jo opened the window and shouted out, "You son of a bitch!" (He never swore.)

This so startled me that I pulled over to the side, stopped the car and said, "I must say that was brilliant. You certainly have come a long way from 'thank you.'"

* * *

The nephews came to dinner and he made a big effort to talk.

"You should be well by Christmas," we all told him, joyfully.

He thanked us.

I saw him leave the room. He was in his study, counting the weeks until Christmas.

I walked in and said, "That's right, darling, you'll be well by Christmas."

He looked at me with large frightened eyes.

"I saw him ticking July off the calendar. August was over but then I caught him drawing a Christmas tree with a question mark in September. When I told him that was cheating, he gave me a marvelous Italian shrug.

* * *

One day, Jennifer Jones appeared, all in white. She had telephoned me in the morning. Having been in Europe, she had not heard about Jo's stroke until the night before.

"Oh, Pat, did Jo have a stroke?" she asked.

I told her that he had, and I also told her about his speech . . . or lack of it.

"Can he see anyone?" she asked

"He can see you," I replied.

"When?"

"Any time," I said.

She came over right away, bringing lovely white orchids to her gardener friend. Jennifer never changes, she is ever beautiful and kind and has become the best organizer in the world.

I remember her handling our wedding with such skill. Then David had died and she had a few years of grieving and loneliness until she met Norton Simon. We had adored

David, and we hated to see her alone for so long. Norton, although unlike David, is strangly similar.

Norton encourages her in all her undertakings, as well he should. This shy, genuine introvert is still shy and introverted, but she works so hard for charities, and her interest in mental health and cancer is unbounded; they must feel better just seeing her enter hospitals and board rooms.

Jo found her very easy to talk to. He had his pad and pencil, but did not have to use them too often. Seeing them together, they looked very much the same as they did in all their movies some years earlier, *Portrait of Jennie, Love Letters, Since You Went Away* — to name a few.

She calmly told us that we had been cooped up too long in our apartment and in hospital rooms, and that she would send a limousine on Sunday to bring us over to their beautiful house in Malibu where we could enjoy the sea air, the change of scenery, and just be with them for as long, or a little as we chose.

We chose to stay all day. It was so refreshing, cozy and totally relaxing.

On Monday, Jo was back to the grindstone. He said he had never worked so hard in his life. Making movies was a breeze compared to this 'born again' necessity.

But he really was too tired to work. That following Sunday, he awakened weak and depressed. After a silent brunch, he went into the den to play his Solitaire. The game did not help his sad mood.

Poor, brave, fighting man. Pity he would not accept. Love and hope were his needs, and I had an abundance of both.

He went out on the terrace, perhaps his trees and flowers would smile upon him. He turned them to face the sun. No smile.

Finally, I went out and looked straight at him and said, "Why are you so sad? You are more tired than you realize. You probably should go back to bed."

"Too much sleep," he said.

"Nonsense," I said. "Rest is important to you as is eating and drinking and working."

"I . . . never get better," he told me in his awkward wording.

"Oh, so that's it," I said. "I've been expecting some kind of reaction, but to tell you the truth, I expected it much earlier, when things looked very precarious, when everything you uttered was wrong. Have you forgotten those days? Don't you realize how you've improved? You seem to come out with a new word each day. That may not sound great, but that's the way it's going to be for the present. You must stumble, make mistakes, try to correct them, and feel stimulated and happy when you get them right. My darling Jo. I never thought you'd give up hope. I love you more than anyone, and my admiration for your bravery and tenacity is unbounded. Don't let us down. Please tell me you'll get better, because I know you will, but I want to hear it from you."

"I . . . better."

"Again," I said.

"I — get — better."

"Again," I said.

"I — will — get better. I — will — get better . . . I — will — *get better*."

I made him sleep some more, and went outside on the terrace alone with my thoughts.

* * *

Orson telephoned. "I'm on my way over."

Jo was nervous, then he remembered Orson's sensitivity as a director and I think he felt calm.

Within a short time, his huge frame filled our living room. I looked at these two friends: the giant with his black cloak, his clear diction with such deep expressive tones; the tall, more delicate one, in his elegant robe and ascot, his hands expressed everything he wrote on a pad.

Orson decided to write, too. They spent the whole afternoon writing notes to each other. Some short, some long and some even illustrated.

Orson decided not to write to me, but to speak. "I'll be back in a few days, Patricia."

I walked to the door with him. He flung his cape round his enormous shoulders, walked out, then turned and said, "I don't have to tell you to look after him, but thank you for loving him so much. I came here to try and help Jo but you two have renewed my faith in love and I'm the one who feels better."

He was gone, but thank God not for long.

* * *

Now Orson's sessions were speaking sessions. Any time Jo stumbled and really messed up a word, Orson would say, "Oh, I like that much better, Jo. I'm going to use it. How does it go again?"

Those therapeutic visits sometimes ended in gales of laughter.

* * *

Jo was not paralyzed at all, but his leg had been bothering him a great deal. When I mentioned this to Douglas, he sent us to a neurologist that he recommended highly. His name was Dr. Woods.

Dr. Woods said that he must exercise that leg for as long and as often as he could.

So I said, "Do you think it would be a good idea if we bought a house in Palm Springs? There he would be able to swim every day."

Dr. Woods said it was the most intelligent idea he'd ever heard. I hadn't expected that answer. However, it did seem to Jo that it was a good idea.

* * *

So, we drove down to Palm Springs. As we arrived in the town, it was getting dark and there were little lights in the trees along Palm Canyon.

We drove very slowly. It was quite romantic. Finding a hotel was easy. We decided to have a candlelight dinner in our room, settle down for the night and, in the morning, get on to an agent and just take a look around.

When we got into bed, I put my head on Jo's shoulder. He said, "Patricia, what a marvelous idea this was."

"Well, darling, I just want to keep you warm," I replied.

He put his arms around me and whispered, "We'll keep each other warm forever."

We have always shared a bed. As Jo had said, when we were first married, "We are together all day, or at least some of it. When we're not together, I miss you but I have the nights to look forward to. I couldn't sleep without you beside me."

Later, we fell asleep . . . together. Always together.

The next day, we looked at several houses. They all had swimming pools and patios and gardens and flowers and the sun was shining. I held Jo's hand and it was warm; his face was aglow. I walked very proudly, cognizant of my brilliant idea.

On our third day of looking at houses, we found a small house in the Las Palmas area — fully furnished — (not too bad) with a small garden, a lovely pool and masses of flower beds. The owners wanted to sell it right away. We bought it, returned to Los Angeles, packed a few things and moved in.

Jo's nephew, Joseph Cotten, ' (we call him "Young Joe"), and his adorable wife Penny, had moved to California. We became their West Coast parents.

Every Saturday after working, they would drive down to Palm Springs and spend the weekend with us. Jo really had more in common with his namesake than anyone else. His father named him well.

Wherever we lived, Joe and Penny would come on Sundays. "Young Joe" would have dinner in the bedroom with his uncle. Penny and I would eat in the dining room. We looked forward to their visits, for they are truly a happy couple and their company and affection cheered and helped Jo.

He would try and tell his nephew funny stories about his grandparents and uncle Whit.

Penny and I would listen to the laughter from the bedroom and we felt very hopeful.

* * *

Jo swam often, very often, and Susie recommended a very fine teacher called Lowell Nece. He gave him speech lessons every day and between swimming and lessons, he really worked hard.

And, do you know something? We were blissfully happy. In fact, we decided to sell our place in Los Angeles and stay in Palm Springs. The sun and the swimming were doing Jo a great deal of good. We were also making a few friends.

* * *

Some people we barely knew invited us to a charity dinner at a big hotel with entertainment. We had become such introverts that the idea seemed wild to us, and we were a little insecure. But, we went.

Sitting nervously at one of the round tables, Jo suddenly got a slap on the back. He looked up into the face of Bob Hope!

"What are you doing here?" asked the world's most beloved comic.

"We live here," answered Jo as Bob ran down to the

Joseph Cotten III and his adorable wife, Penny.

stage. As he walked or glided or strutted (whatever he uses for movement) to the center of the stage, he said, "Ladies and gentlemen, we have among us tonight one of America's finest actors, Joseph Cotten. Jo stand up and let everyone see you."

Jo slowly stood up and I could see the glow as the applause started and he took a bow and gazed with such gratitude at the brilliant gentleman on stage.

* * *

Hope springs eternal. May it be ever thus. Of course, now I realize Bob doesn't glide or strut, he springs. From war to war, from country to country, he takes his message of love and laughter. He is the greatest ambassador on this planet.

Behind every great man there is a woman. In this case 'beside' is a better description of Hope's wife. When she is beside him he shines with pride and with good reason. I am proud to call Dolores a friend. I don't have to know when she is in Palm Springs, I sense it. It's in the air. The quail trot to a different beat when she is there, and the hummingbirds hum a more joyful refrain.

I have friends that I have known much longer, that I value greatly and I believe in loyalty to them all, so I have no right or reason to claim such distinctive knowledge about Dolores. But I do claim it, for the simple reason that she has a presence which is rare and that presence is felt by many people. I suspect that her husband was the first to notice it many years ago.

It is needless to add that our visits to their home, be it to a small dinner or a large party, were for us an "event."

* * *

One afternoon the telephone rang and a voice I didn't recognize said, "Mrs. Cotten?"

"Yes, who is this?"

"My name is David Gest. I am starting an awards celebration yearly and I would like your husband to accept the first award."

"Mr. Gest, my husband has been extremely ill for a long time. His recovery is very slow, indeed, so it would be quite impossible for him to accept your award — much as I'm sure he'd like to."

"I'm not giving the awards until October. He'll be fine by then, I'm sure."

His marvelously optimistic attitude impressed me but I couldn't get Jo into something that he'd be either too nervous to do or completely unable. His health was so precious.

"Well, I sincerely hope you're right. That would be wonderful but I'm afraid I cannot commit him for any personal appearance. So, you'll have to forgive me but thank you, anyway."

"I'm not accepting 'no' for an answer either — I'll call you in a few weeks. Give him my best wishes. He's a wonderful actor."

I said, "Thank you," but he had hung up!

Some weeks later the same young man called again. This time I recognized his voice.

"I'm calling to ask you and your husband to have lunch with me. I know he's been out. How about lunch tomorrow?"

"Mr. Gest, don't you realize you are calling Palm Springs?"

"Yes, I have a house here. I just want you to have lunch with me tommorow. I'll pick you up at twelve-thirty." End of conversation.

We went to lunch with him. He was extremely young and thoroughly persistent. Jo told him, and, of course, he realized, that Jo had a speech problem. "All that you need to say is 'thank you'," said David.

"I'll try," said Jo, in his dry way.

We didn't realize what we were getting into, but it turned out to be a remarkably stimulating, interesting and rewarding few years.

* * *

The American Cinema Awards started fairly small, but, within the first five years, reached tremendous heights.

Jo had only ladies introduce him — Teresa Wright, who was so great with Jo in *Shadow of A Doubt,* came from New York to hand him the Award; after, Jennifer made a speech about all the movies they made together; then, Dorothy Maguire spoke about all the movies they hadn't done together! — but they were very good friends. It was Butterfly McQueen who stole the show by saying sadly in that inimitable voice that she wished she'd had had more scenes with Jo in *Gone With The Wind.* She obviously couldn't remember doing any scenes with Jo in *Gone With The Wind* because he wasn't in the movie! Joel McCrea received a well-deserved award, as did his lovely wife, Frances Dee. Angie Dickinson was the mistress of ceremonies. Milton Berle made a typical Milton Berle speech. It was a good evening.

David then asked Jo and me if we would become Co-Chairs for the American Cinema Awards. We agreed and found ourselves in one of the most original charity events each year.

The money we made went to the Motion Picture Country House. A few of us would drive there after each show and I would deliver the check.

The Beverly Wilshire Hotel Ballroom was attractively decorated for the events. The dinners were served before we started. Two hundred stars appeared at most events, so we had to move to the Hilton Hotel, which had considerably more space.

The entertainment was always terrific: Robert Goulet sang his heart out — what a lovely voice; Rosemary Clooney, who gets better every year, gave us songs with her fantastic rhythm; Donald O'Connor and Debbie Reynolds performed beautifully together; and, as the years went on, the shows got better and we certainly had no trouble getting great performers.

Of course, I most certainly am not forgetting the Awards given for acting: One year, we had Clint Eastwood; then we had Deborah Kerr, who came from Switzerland; Olivia de Havilland, who came from France; Lauren Bacall, who came from New York; Anabella (looking ageless) came from France; and, Mr. Sinatra came from Palm Springs — he was witty and emotional. Liza Minnelli kissed him and called him "Uncle Frank." If I mention all the awards, I'll have to write another book . . . Of course Greg Peck, and Michael Douglas, who thanked his father and his beautiful stepmother. Did I forget Bette Davis? I'll never forget her. Sophia Loren came with Michael Jackson.

All the M.G.M. crowd were very popular: June Allyson, Margaret O'Brien, Ann Rutherford and then some. Shirley Temple was awarded for obvious reasons. Marion Lederer watched her marvelous actor-husband Francis receive an award.

Awards were given for music. Jo and I were delighted to meet Julio Iglesias. He and I had a warm conversation in Spanish. The following day he sent me eight million roses! I kept the card and have all his records!

We wanted to give Jennifer (Jones) an award but she couldn't leave Norton, who was quite ill. We did give one to Jimmy Stewart.

The most unusual and moving part of all the evenings' entertainment was that David brought in actors who were able to come from the Motion Picture Home. Robert Wagner would walk onto the stage and call out all the names of the celebrities; some, who thought they were forgotten; some, who are working non-stop today. As they were called, they stood and a huge light shone on their old and young faces and everyone of them looked beautiful in the glow that was a compliment to their talent.

My darling Jo was getting weaker, but he managed to accompany me every time to the Awards. We always gave a cocktail buffet in a smaller room for those out-of-towners and any near-locals who arrived the day before. I would give a little welcoming speech for those who had travelled. Every time a lady came to our table, Jo said, "Please forgive me. I cannot stand up safely." He disliked not being a gentleman more than he hated admitting that he was having difficulty walking.

A great deal of hard work was involved and wonderful Leo Jaffe, Head of Columbia Pictures, took over from us as Jo got weaker. Leo did a great job — more Palm Springs' friends came through him: Anita Jaffe, Leo's wife, Marion and Jack Shea (whom Jo admired immensely), Marisa and James Shea (no relation), and many more. Leo as Chairman and beautiful Anne Douglas hostessing was a great combination. Dr. Reza Masaheri, the great Palm Springs plastic surgeon, came with some very beautiful ladies. They didn't seem to mind our looking at them. They knew we were envious.

That young Mr. Gest could one day be a great impresario. I wish him well. He has the talent and the energy.

- 17 -

The World is Topsy Turvy

Piti called and told me that Daddy had died. He had had heart trouble for some time. Jo came and held me close as I cried my heart out. "We must get over and see the family," he said.

"Jo, darling, you cannot take the trip. You've had a massive stroke and I can't go without you because I won't leave you. Let's walk to the little church around the corner and say a prayer for him."

"You go now, darling. I'm awfully slow, so I'll come with my stick and I'll join you."

Half an hour later, Jo was standing outside the church, leaning on his stick with a limousine parked beside him. "Get in," he said. "I have plenty of medication and our tickets. I did talk to Douglas. I can go along as well, if we come back right after you've seen Piti, Gloria and your mother."

I got in the limousine, Jo put his arms around me and kissed my tear-stained face.

Once on the plane, I gave him his medicine and he fell asleep. I leaned against his shoulder and thought about my rare, brilliant, intellectual and, of course, musical father. I could hear him singing "Nessun Dorma" from Puccini's *Turandot*, standing at La Scala, Milan; I could hear the applause. His God-given voice drowned out the sound of the plane and filled my heart with love and pride and regret for not being able to kiss him goodbye.

It was a long trip filled with half-dreams and occasional grateful looks at the pale face of my beloved husband.

Gloria and Gerry met us and said that Piti and Ken had not slept all day and night for almost a week. They had been at the hospital sitting beside Daddy until he died. He had been slipping away quietly, but they revived him in the ambulance; that sadly kept him alive and tossing in a fitful coma until the end, so he did not go gentle into that good night.

Gloria also said that Piti and Ken were taking Daddy to be buried with his Spanish family. She advised me wisely to stay with her and Mummy while they took the trip. "Pat, you're an actress and I don't think you should arrive like the heroine and take the credit."

Of course, she was right. I had no intention of going, nor was I going to leave Jo.

The night before they left, Piti and I talked long into the night about our childhood. In the morning, my tired and responsible sister and Ken caught the plane and took dear Daddy to sleep with his family.

Mummy couldn't go. She had developed Parkinson's. Gloria and Gerry had bought a larger house in the country still in Beaconsfield. They took Mummy to live with them for the rest of her life. They gave her a lovely room with a large bay window overlooking the copper beach trees and the flowers on the lawn. It faced south, so that the demur English sun would sporadically brighten her outlook, while Gloria with her perfectly trained coloratura would sing to her from *La Boheme, Tosca* and *Madame Butterfly.*

Piti and Ken returned to London — Ken to his piano and Brahms and Chopin. Music had always been in their life and would remain so.

* * *

Mummy began to get worse. I kept in constant touch with Piti.

At the same time, my Jo began getting weaker; travelling was now out of the question. Then, the second call came — Piti said, "It's happened."

Mummy, brave, witty and beautiful — the best mother in the world — gave in quietly while holding Gloria's hand. Poor little Gloria was distraught.

I dream about Mummy often, and Piti has told me that she dreams about her, too. Gloria, I'm sure, thinks about her constantly. She was the baby, and she had Mummy living with her for several years. For this, I must thank my brother-in-law Gerry. It couldn't have been easy for him to have an old lady in his house all the time and his wife and daughter ministering to her — even if she was his mother-in-law — but, Gerry loved her and she loved him. Together, they made her last few years as comfortable and as loving as possible.

* * *

We three have been very lucky in our marriages.

Piti and Ken still behave as they did when they were first married — they argue constantly and they love each other while they argue. They never bore each other, they have a lot in common and they are great parents. Jennifer, their daughter, and Christopher, their son, each are happily married and have children of their own.

Gloria and Gerry are a fun couple. I think their love has grown through the years. They are such good company and entertain beautifully. They have a son, Michael, a fine product of Harrow School. Stephanie, their daughter, is my little pet. She is very attractive and has her mother's sense of humor. She is married and they have a daughter whom I have not yet seen — but, from her pictures, she is adorable.

So now, we get to Patricia Medina-Cotten and the one and only, Joseph Cotten. I have written a lot about Jo. I have mentioned his bravery, his rare dry humor, his fine looks, his sensitivity, and as much as you should know about his sexuality. You do not know enough about his generosity, therefore, I think you should read this!

* * *

Richard Greene's best friend, Michael Graham, called me in Palm Springs from England. He wondered if I could speak to Frank McCarthy as he was highly important in the Screen Actors Guild. He said he was sure Richard was owed a pension and maybe Frank could help him get it.

I asked him if Richard had a problem because I knew he had made a lot of money, and certainly more than a million on Robin Hood. Michael said Richard had invested very badly trying to start a new series, and he'd also lost a lot of money training horses. Richard's wife had separated from him and kept the house, and he was living in the north of England in a tiny cottage. He'd had a serious accident and couldn't work. Earlier he had come to see me in Mexico. He wanted to be a success on the English stage—he suffered from the same problems as I. I had wanted to do comedy, and he wanted to do Shakespeare.

While this sad conversation was going on, Jo was doing one of his many hobbies — gold-leaf work — in the hall. I told him I was going to call Frank about the Guild, but I didn't hold much hope as they had already been spoken to.

Jo walked up to me and handed me an envelope. "I think you'd better write the letter. There's a check inside."

"Jo, you don't have to do anything about this," I said.

"You have always remained friends with him. It sounds to me as if he's in a bad way. Write him a note from both of us. That check should help him. I certainly hope it does."

Richard wrote as soon as he received it and said he couldn't have managed without it. He was overwhelmed by the generous check. He could now go to a clinic in Switzerland where he had been told they could heal the wounds from his accident.

I kissed Jo and said, "You are the kindest man in the world."

He held me closer than close. "I have the world in my arms," he whispered as he stroked my hair.

* * *

Jo couldn't work. That was out of the question, even though he was beginning to speak quite clearly now. He was about 95 percent cured and going to lunches. Reading scripts was fun for him, and he had been sent many.

All were turned down because as he put it, "I was a very good actor. I am not going to be anything other than a good actor. I simply couldn't bear to let anyone hear me stumbling over my dialogue on the set. They would feel sorry for me and I wouldn't blame them. I'm finished and that's that."

What a sad statement to make. Yet, he was right. Although he could carry on a conversation, and sometimes that spark would come in his eye and he couldn't control his wicked wit, learning a part was quite a different burden. One he was not yet ready to carry.

Once he was sent a script with quite easy dialogue. He read it several times and reluctantly refused it.

They came back saying they could make it easier and use words he could learn.

"We will send you another script. We'll cut anything you don't want to say. In fact, we'd work you just a short time."

He looked at me. I could see the excitement in his face. I called Lowell Nece, his speech therapist. He came over every day and they began working on the scenes Jo would be doing in the picture.

After each session, Jo was completely exhausted. This began to worry me. I didn't want to tell him he couldn't do it, but I was dreadfully fearful. After about two weeks, his voice became faint. He started pushing it. I called Dr. Gatto, the throat doctor in Palm Springs, and took Jo to his office to have him looked at.

"His throat looks like raw hamburger," said Dr. Gatto, who apparently didn't believe in euphemisms. "I don't like it at all," he added. "Also, he has severe laryngitis."

I drove him home in silence. As we reached the gate, Jo whispered:

"I can't do the film, please get me out of it, darling."

He had made the decision himself, but at what cost?

I told Lowell it was impossible; he was not surprised. Then I called his agent and told him to tell the producers the truth. They had been wonderfully kind and patient and deserved to know immediately so they could cast someone else, Burt Lancaster played the part.

Jo stayed in bed a couple of days. It didn't do him any good, and when he did say a few words, his voice was high and sounded painful. Bed, and my nursing, were not the answer.

I telephoned Dr. Forde and put Jo on the phone. He said a couple of words and handed it back to me.

"Bring him into St. John's tomorrow. We'll have Dr. Hutcherson look at him in the hospital, and I'll also have a lung man there."

St. John's became our second home. My poor Jo had been speaking so awfully well. Now something else had happened. What could it be? Why, oh why did his laryngitis get increasingly worse? How much could one take?

What were they going to do? It was getting so late.

I was hoping wonderful Virginia Zamboni, the Executive Vice President at St. John's for 17 years, would come and see us.

From early in the morning until late in the afternoon, we had been there. Jo did his crossword puzzle rather as if he were waiting for a train. I sat and thought.

At about five o'clock, Virginia came in and said, "They're not going to let Jo out of the hospital tonight. It's too late and with his history, they want to put him in a room. Are you going back to the hotel, Pat?"

"Yes. I wish you could join me for dinner."

"I most certainly will," she said. "I'm not letting you drive tonight."

"Thank you," whispered Jo.

They came. He was given a shot. Douglas took his pulse and blood pressure, and then checked his lungs (which he'd already x-rayed).

"Douglas, will you be with me?" whispered Jo.

"Of course, and I'm not leaving the hospital until I know everything tonight."

He put his arm 'round Jo's thin shoulders and Jo smiled and gave a sigh of relief.

"We'll have to wait a few minutes more," said Douglas.

Jo was woozy from the medication. He reached out for my hand and whispered in his falsetto voice:

"Do you remember when we got into a taxi late at night in New York and I told the driver where to go?"

No reply. I knew what was coming:

"Remember," he said, "I can't see you but I'm sure you're Joseph Cotten, I'd know that voice anywhere." He dropped my hand, closed his eyes and they wheeled him out. I remembered.

There would be a cardiologist, naturally an anesthetist, the lung man, Douglas, and the surgeon, Dr. Hutcherson.

I sat for a long time. Virginia popped in occasionally to see how I was. Good people

My dear friend Virginia Zamboni.

do not usually make the newsstands. Virginia is innately good and deserves more than a mention on these pages. There should be a Virginia in every hospital everywhere (God willing).

After what seemed an eternity, they came back, except Jo. Dr. Hutcherson spoke:

* * *

"Now, there's a little something there. I've removed a bit but it's not cancer, so it won't be too serious."

For the first time I wanted to kiss him.

Virginia drove me to the hotel. We clinked glasses, drank to Jo's health and ordered a fine dinner.

"I'll come and pick you up in the morning," said Virginia.

"I will not have it, I'll take a taxi. My car is at the hospital and Jo and I can get on the freeway home from there."

The head waiter came over and told me I was wanted on the telephone. I walked across the long room and picked up the phone.

"Patricia," said Douglas, "I'm afraid Jo has cancer of the vocal chords."

"He can't have. Dr. Hutcherson said it wasn't that. There's been some mistake."

"I have just seen the biopsy. Now I'll meet you at 7:00 A.M. and we'll have to go and tell him, . . Patricia?"

I dropped the phone . . . I walked toward our table. Virginia got up and took hold of me.

She took me up to my room and I screamed and cried, and cried and screamed. I don't remember Virginia leaving.

At about 1:30 A.M., I called my sister Piti in England. I could hardly talk. She offered to come over. I said it wouldn't help Jo. I don't know what else I said. I hung up. I threw up, and finally I lay still on the bed and all I could hear was my very strong heartbeat. My tears had stopped but my heart was crying.

* * *

I got up, had a cold shower and tried to make my eyes look less swollen, for Jo and then I took a taxi to St. John's Hospital. I went straight to Virginia's office.

She said, "I'll call Dr. Forde and ask him to meet us in the commissary. We could all use a cup of coffee."

The three of us had our coffee, then Dr. Forde took my arm and said, "Let's go."

Virginia came with us but stayed outside in the corridor. We walked in and looked at the bed. It was empty. Jo was seated in a chair, completely dressed, with his smart blazer and ascot on. His beautiful hair combed and shining.

Douglas spoke, "Has the surgeon been in?"

"Yes," squeaked Jo.

"Did he say anything?"

"He said I have cancer." Then he looked at me. "I'm awfully sorry, darling, you'll have to take me to lots of treatments."

I couldn't say anything.

"Well, I'm ready, let's go."

The nurse came in with a wheelchair, but Virginia rushed in and took it from her. Jo sat in it and she started wheeling him away.

I looked at Douglas and said, "Do you believe his bravery? I was quite stunned."

"So was I," he said. "But there's only one Joseph Cotten."

He certainly never spoke truer words. I felt ashamed of my hysterics.

* * *

I raced after the wheelchair, got my car out of the parking lot, and Virginia helped him in.

"Are the treatments going to be at the Desert Hospital?"

"Yes."

"Then I really don't think either of us is up to that drive today. Let's go back to the hotel, have lunch and take a long nap. We'll leave tomorrow and start on your cure."

We each had a glass of wine, and I ordered lunch as if we hadn't a care in the world. After lunch we went upstairs and both fell into bed, exhausted, desperate and lost.

"You'll get well, darling," I said.

"Yes . . . I will."

I kissed his forehead and we went to sleep.

* * *

We drove back to the desert, having been told to contact a Dr. Eades at the Desert Hospital. Dr. Eades was said to be an expert on radiation. I telephoned him on arriving home, and he said he'd like to see us both the following morning at 10:00 A.M.

We went to the hospital and were sent down to a large basement where Dr. Eades held consultations and several people gave the radiation treatments.

Dr. Eades was a tall, fine looking man with an easy personality. He had had cancer himself. How long ago, I do not know. He took us into a room and spoke to us for about an hour. He showed us rather explicit models of throats and vocal chords and gave us many books to take home and study.

Before we left, he gave Jo a thorough examination and said he would require thirty-four radiation treatments on his vocal chords starting at 1:00 P.M. the following day. After the treatments were completed, we were to see a throat specialist every three months for five years, unless it broke out before that. Then he could have no more radiation, and the next step was unbearable and we both decided unacceptable.

We cancelled all our dates. My daily girl, Robin, was pregnant with her second child and the doctor had advised her to stop work for some time.

The treatments would make Jo very weak. He was told to rest a lot and take a lot of nourishment. Jo told me that Thomas Jefferson only went into the kitchen to wind up the clock. But Thomas Jefferson had slaves. He also was the first person to bring a waffle iron over here from France in the 1700's!

I had no slaves and certainly no waffle iron. So I was lucky indeed in getting a new wonderful housekeeper named Vilma. Jo could not swallow anything hard, and, in between meals, he was told to have malted milk with an egg in it. Fortunately, he adored malted milk and ice cream, but anything too hot or too cold was not allowed. I asked Dr. Eades if he could have a glass of wine with his evening meal.

"Oh, heavens yes. Poor fellow, he's having an awful time. He'll need it."

* * *

Jo would not allow himself to have an awful time. He rested very little. He did his crosswords and played his Solitaire.

Every day at 1:00 P.M., we went to the hospital. Sometimes we had to wait and we'd see such frail people come out. The good doctor and his assistant were always cheerful and smiling.

While waiting for Jo to have his treatment, I would talk to the other patients.

* * *

A young man was there several times. He was painfully thin and had blotches on his face. One day after he had been sitting in his chair asleep, he opened his eyes, looked at me and said, "I'm so sorry to have been sleeping. I just felt so tired."

I said, "Oh, don't apologize. I know how dreadfully weakening radiation can be. Please sleep if you want to. They'll call when they are ready."

He moved a little. "It isn't the radiation that leaves me totally weak. You see, I have AIDS."

"I'm so sorry," I said.

"I'm going to lick it, and when I do I shall lead a completely different life. Do you think I'll get better?"

I looked at this forlorn, pathetic and very ill young man and said, I hoped convincingly, "Yes, if you are determined and do everything the doctors say and pray a lot, yes I think and hope that you will get better."

At that moment, Jo came out and I introduced them. They shook hands and he told Jo how much he enjoyed his acting.

In the car, Jo said, "That poor young man. He does look so terribly ill."

"He has AIDS, " I said.

"How do you know?"

"We talked."

The next day, we talked some more, and the third day, his brother brought him, and we all talked. The young man was noticeably weaker.

He said, "My brother is cross with me because I haven't got the strength to shave."

"This is his last treatment," said the brother, after the boy had gone into the surgery. "They cannot do anymore for him. He asked me to give you this note."

I did not read it until I got home. It was just a little scrawl thanking me for befriending him. Poor little fellow. He needed love so much. I really believe his brother loved him and was looking after him, but . . .

We never saw him again. We saw older people with cancer suffering so much. Most of them either had a healthy husband or wife or some family member with them who seemed to care.

Oh, how much they were needed.

They were all interested in seeing Jo there. He spent time talking to them, sharing their problems. He knew when to just listen, when to answer their questions, when to give sympathy and when a touch of humor was needed to lift their spirits.

- 18 -

LOVE is a Four-Letter Word

Every night before we settled down, I asked Jo, "Are you all right?"

The answer had always been, "Yes."

Then one night, when I asked, "Are you all right?"

"No. I feel as if I'm going to have another stroke. My head is going round and round."

Immediately, I dialed 911 for the paramedics and the ambulance. They came in no time at all. They were much quicker than the Los Angeles crew.

They put him on a stretcher, took him to the ambulance and said they would take him to Emergency at the Desert Hospital.

"Do you want to follow us?"

In an instant, I was in my car and we were off on the short trip to the hospital.

It was 3:00 A.M. and this was Saturday! Going through the town took forever. The young people were out of school, they had been drinking and taking whatever they should have said no to. The girls were as bad as the boys, taking off their clothes and jumping into jeeps belonging to complete strangers. They couldn't have remained strangers for long.

The siren blared forth. I followed a foot behind them. We finally arrived at the Emergency. Jo was removed from his stretcher and put into a room full of beds. One cubicle was empty and in they took him.

A very nice doctor spoke to him and then to me.

"Do you have a physician I can speak to?" he asked.

I produced my telephone book which is ever with me. "If you let me use the telephone, I'll try and get him for you."

Poor Dr. Forde. I have no sympathy for him on occasions like these; I *need* him. So, at 3:30 A.M., a sleepy voice answered my ringing. He spoke to me seriously and kindly.

"I'm sure he's not having another stroke. It's something to do with the position of his neck while sleeping. Let me speak to the doctor and tell him what medication to give him, if he has not already done so."

I called the nice doctor. They spoke for awhile, then Douglas asked to speak to me again.

"He agrees with me and, in fact, has already started him on the medication. It should have its effect in an hour or so. Please call me in just over an hour."

"They don't want me to stay in here. Shall I wait outside?"

"No. If you are there you'll see that they get on with it."

"The squeaky wheel?" I asked.

"Um hm," said our physician as he hung up the telephone.

The doctor said, "I have not yet admitted your husband into the hospital. I'll take you to the office where you must give the lady all the information she needs."

* * *

She was a sweet, gentle, little old lady who had no right being up at that hour.

"Sit down, dear," she said as she picked out a pen and a sheet of paper.

"The name I know," she said in a quavery voice, "but I need to have his Social Security number."

"Shit!" came a shout from behind my back. "What the fuck good is this hospital?"

"His Social Security number, please," she said softly.

An arm, bleeding slightly, was flung over my shoulder.

"Silly old bitch, I'm bleeding to death and what are you doing — this is the worst hospital I've ever been to. Now answer me! What the fuck are you going to do about it?"

Looking up, she straightened her little glasses and in a voice as loud as Bette Midler's she stormed, "I'll tell you what I'm going to do about it. I'm going to call security and have you fucking well thrown out of here." With a dainty veined finger she pushed a bell.

The young man's friend appeared and grabbed him, muttering something. They were both obviously stoned.

"Now, how old is Mr. Cotten?" asked Grandma Moses, having returned to her sweet nature.

The young man was removed by security and attended to in another part of the forest.

I went back to see my Jo in his very small cubicle, and at the appointed hour, I called Douglas.

Some time later on, Jo was released with his medication that he was to be kept on for three days, by which time, he would be pronounced well.

"Please don't pick a weekend to get sick again."

"I'll try not to. Was it very upsetting for you?"

"Yes, it *fucking* well was," I heard myself say to a completely startled husband.

But, so typical of Jo, he never mentioned it. He presumed that I was tired and frightened and did not realize what I was saying. In a way, he was right. I was still in shock, not only by the niagara of four-letter words that I had been exposed to; it was a delayed shock. At the time, my mind was entirely on Jo and his fear of another stroke.

My faith in Douglas' telephonic diagnosis had eased me enormously. Then I was confronted with a damaged vein and a filthy brain. However, thinking about it later, I realized the poor young man was out of his mind on drugs, and I hated whoever had given them to him. The little old lady really had stunned me, and that gave me food for serious guessing about her status there. Had she maybe once been a policewoman, and in later years, volunteered to work weekends at the Hospital? I never found out, but I did hear that the young man's bleeding had been successfully attended to.

All this, of course, Jo had been unaware of, lying in his pristine, pure white sheets, trying to get well.

* * *

Now we had to face having Jo's throat checked every so often by a throat specialist.

We had used Dr. Gatto in Palm Springs several times. He was a very able throat doctor, and each time we'd been, since the surgeon at St. John's, he said everything looked all right. So we went to see him again — this time his attitude was quite different.

"I'm not happy about him. I think you should call Dr. Forde to arrange for Jo to see a man who specializes in the larynx. I don't want to frighten you, but I don't like the look of it. I think it should be checked thoroughly."

We called Douglas and he said he'd call us back. He had been working on who Jo should go to.

He called and said that he had come to the conclusion that a man with a very fine reputation was at UCLA. His name was Dr. Calcaterra. Douglas had made an appointment for Jo to see him the next day.

* * *

We drove into Los Angeles and kept our appointment. We had to wait such a long time. It was on the seventh floor and I think it was called the "Head and Neck Clinic." There were so many people with dreadful things wrong with them also waiting.

We went to see Dr. Calcaterra. He was a very busy man. There were several doctors, they were all busy, but they gave us a smile, and one patted Jo on the shoulder.

Finally, we were called into Dr. Calcaterra's office. He apparently was *extra* busy and his time with us was, to phrase it kindly, "very limited." He looked down Jo's throat and said, "I need a biopsy," then he left . . . this was our Patient/Doctor introduction!

Jo was put into the hospital right away and given a biopsy.

A doctor who worked with the "Great Doctor" said that I was to go down and sit in the crowded lobby and wait for Calcaterra to telephone me. Usually, the doctors had asked me to wait in the quiet of Jo's room, so at least I could pray — or cry. However, my comfort was of no importance to me. I was there to be with my husband when he wasn't in surgery, to presumably have a discussion with the surgeon and to help Jo go through any treatments and suffering.

After looking at all the worried faces for a seemingly long time, the lady at the telephone said Dr. Calcaterra was on the line. I fled to the telephone. He said he was not pleased with the biopsy. He wanted to use a laser and do several other biopsies. I agreed to the laser, but told him if he found anything else to do nothing until he had discussed it with Jo.

When Jo came to, we went home. We were to wait a few weeks before returning for more research. We did not see the doctor before the operation.

Back I went to the crowded, nerve-wracking lobby. I suppose I could have gone to Jo's room and left a message for the doctor to call me there. It would have been just as easy for him — but, I would have waited in a cellar if it could help my Jo. I sat there wondering and waiting, praying silently and incessantly.

"Mrs. Cotten," said the lady at the desk. She didn't have to explain any further.

In a second, I grabbed the telephone.

"I have news for you, the cancer has spread into the muscles. Laser is no good at all. As a matter of fact, your husband is a candidate for a total laryngectomy, not a partial. He's now in recovery, so we'll talk about it when he comes round."

I dropped the phone. I ran through the halls of UCLA, into the elevator and up to Jo's room, flung myself across the bed and let go. Unsuccessfully, trying to control myself, I called Dr. Forde's office. The nurse was most upset at my hysterics and said Douglas was in the building in another doctor's office and she'd call him right away. Meantime, she wanted to keep me on the telephone and try and calm me down. I hung up.

Still in an uncontrollable state, I got in my car and drove to Forde's office.

He let me weep my heart out. I couldn't stop.

Finally, he said, "Now tell me everything."

I blurted it all out in fury; my fury was violent. I kept saying, "I won't have it. It's not fair. He should have checked sooner."

He agreed that it wasn't fair, that we should get other opinions, and that I should try very hard to be calm for Jo's sake. After all, he didn't know anything yet.

When I pulled myself together, Douglas saw me to my car and I drove back to UCLA to Jo's room to await his arrival from recovery; recovery?

When he was wheeled in, he greeted me with a happy smile.

I knew I had to tell him the awful result as gently as I possibly could before Dr. Calcaterra came in and laid it bluntly on the line.

"I will not have a total laryngectomy," he said softly.

* * *

Dr. Calcaterra came into Jo's room. He sat down and actually made quite a long speech. He said he wanted to operate on Jo for a partial laryngectomy and made a date for a week on Monday, to perfom the operation. Jo told him we were going to get other opinions.

The doctor repeated, "I would like to perform the operation myself."

Douglas came out with many suggestions for second opinions. There apparently was an excellent surgeon at Sloane Kettering in New York, one Dr. Sessions.

We came home. A helpless couple.

"If I have a partial, I may not live very long, but that is my choice."

How could I agree with him? I have always wanted and needed him for ever — love such as ours is selfish. It is a part of oneself.

"It is better to have loved and lost than never to have loved at all."

Years ago I would have agreed with that saying. Now I envy people who love a little, who love enough, and even those whose caring is such that they do not depend upon each other and being apart is part of their life . . . and Death??

The telephone rang. I recognized the voice immediately.

"Pat. It's Jennifer. Is Jo going to have an operation?"

I told her the whole story.

"If only I could get some advice from some knowledgeable and uninvolved source."

"Leave it to me, I'll call you back," said the best friend two people ever had.

She called me back many times and she talked to many influential people. She called Mrs. Lasker and spoke to Dr. Vincent de Vita who, at the time, was the Chief Physician at Sloane Kettering. She also made it possible for me to have a conversation with him.

Dr. de Vita was the most comforting, interesting, calm voice. He said, "If I had your husband's voice, I would cling to it. It's so rare and so beautiful." He told me that Dr. Sessions was an expert on partials, but that he was away in Hong Kong for a while. He thought that Dr. Calcaterra was right in not wanting Jo to wait for a partial.

"He is an excellent surgeon, but your husband should do what he feels strongly about. If a partial laryngectomy gives him one or two more years of his own weak voice, he should decide on that. A total one can be faced later. Remember, it is your husband who makes the decision. Dr. Calcaterra has been down there twice already." He wished us luck.

Everything became clear. Jo had to have his way and leave the rest to the doctors.

We knew an English actor named Jack Hawkins who had a lovely voice but he had to have his larynx removed. He was given a thing round his neck and had a fake voice that was quite frightening and most disturbing to him. He was so unhappy that he didn't take care and was happy to die.

Dr. Calcaterra had said, "I can give you exactly the same voice as Jack Hawkins."

I had heard a few on the same floor as Jo. It broke my heart.

Jo told Calcaterra that, rather than that, he would not speak at all. Just write — or fade away.

* * *

On April 9th, 1989, I checked myself into the Beverly Crest Hotel then drove Jo down to UCLA and checked him in there.

The operation was to be at dawn the next day. Douglas Forde met us there and helped Jo fill in the form permitting the surgery. On our way there, Jo had said to me, "Do you think Douglas is wavering? I hope he doesn't stop my having a partial."

"We'll soon know. He's meeting us there," said I, also dubious.

We should have known better. When it came to filling in the document, Jo signed "Partial Laryngectomy" then looked at Douglas and said, "Is that clear?"

"Why don't you put Partial Laryngectomy *only*," said Douglas.

Jo smiled at his dedicated physician.

I stayed with Jo until 1:00 A.M. when he agreed to take a sleeping pill. They would awaken him at 5:00 A.M., as the surgery was to be at 6:30 A.M.

It was a big and very long operation. When he came back, he was very sick indeed and had an infection. He had a private nurse and he couldn't talk. Also, he had a trach inserted in his throat.

I sat day after day with him just waiting for him to feel better.

He'd look at me. He spoke with his eyes and then he'd rest again. He was so full of medications. He barely knew I was there, except for an occasional smile of reassurance.

* * *

There was a knock at the door. No one was allowed in, so both the nurse and I were startled. She opened the door a little, I was beside her. What I saw didn't really register for a little while.

A beautiful lady stood in the passage not too close to the door. She seemed to be a vision in lilac. Her face was shining, her hair was dark, she had a white long scarf over the lilac suit and I thought I saw wings. She smiled and beckoned to me. Oh my God!

"Jennifer," I said. "You can't see Jo."

"I know that. I've come to take you out to tea."

I walked out and closed the door softly, still unsure whether she was real or a vision.

"Listen, Pat," she said as we got to the elevator. "You have to get out of here once in a while. You need it and Jo needs it."

She was speaking from experience. Norton had suffered from a terrible illness, had fought as bravely as any person could, and through sheer willpower, had overcome hospitalization and was now at home recovering from insurmountable odds. He is a monument to courage and Jennifer was his inspiration. She had learned how often her presence was needed and that sometimes it was good to bring him news from places and people that he didn't see much. He was busy with his board meetings and searching for and finding new artists and older ones.

Jennifer, aside from volunteer work for the disabled, had recently been made Chairman of the Norton Simon Museum by her husband. He had trained her well and he was aware that she was now able to cope with that awesome task.

Do not for one second imagine that Jennifer and I did anything as natural as sipping weak tea and eating thin bread and butter. Oh, no! If this was to be *my* therapy, it had to be far removed from hospital diets or "Ladies Teas." It had to be special and memorable.

We started with a little glass of sherry. Then, out of the choice of teas, we chose "English Breakfast" tea. It had more zip to it. Tiny smoked salmon sandwiches, caviar and toast. These delicacies were followed by homemade scones with clotted cream and strawberry jam.

Upon finishing, we ordered the whole meal over again.

This faintly surprised the waiter, even the first time we did it.

* * *

You see, it was such a cathartic that this "happening" was repeated twice a week the whole time that Jo was in the hospital.

The conversations were extremely important too. We talked about Jo and Norton. We talked about our youth and how long we had all known each other. Happy times, sad times, party times, and work times.

We always ended up deciding that this present time in our lives was happy.

On returning to Jo's hospital room, as soon as he awakened, he would write on his slate (he was not yet speaking).

"A report on the 'tea' please."

Our 'old and restful' feasts had a most cheering effect on Jo.

- 19 -

Home is Best

When I finally got Jo home, still tube feeding after a second long and awful operation, we more or less turned the house into a hospital. We had all his equipment for his I.V., food, etc., including a hospital bed.

In the afternoon, about four o'clock, he would have his much-needed rest, and I would be less than honest if I didn't daydream about tea and sherry and the rest of the nectar, and our harmless and humorous conversations.

Dear Jennifer, you helped Jo's recovery and my sanity. Thank you for your sensitivity and your eternal friendship.

* * *

We had been in our "home hospital" for about two weeks. Jo was in the hospital bed, with me in a single bed beside his machinery, his long pole with his food bag hung on the other side of his bed and every six hours I had to fill it up with another can of Osmolite still being fed through his nose.

I suddenly started shivering uncontrollably. I got up and took my temperature. It was 103 degrees and going up. I grabbed three Keflex from the night table, swallowed them immediately, then went into *our* room and telephoned 911. I told them to send an ambulance for me as I had pneumonia. (I remembered Jo's shivering some years before.)

It was a weekend, and Vilma, our new housekeeper, had weekends off. I telephoned her at home and asked her if she would come over and look after Jo as I had to go to the hospital.

She arrived at about the same time as paramedics came to cart me away. But Jo, ill as he was, noticed my empty little bed and got up bringing his stand with his bag of food on it.

The paramedics said gently, "Come along, Mr. Cotten. We'll get you to the hospital right away."

I came staggering in wearing slacks and a T-shirt and said, "I'm the patient."

"What about him?" said one of the paramedics, gazing at this obviously seriously-ill man.

"He's had an operation and is being looked after. Now, let's go. I want to get back to him."

Vilma tried to get Jo to go to bed, but he stood staring at me desperately with tears in his eyes.

I was determined to be treated and return to him as soon as possible.

The ambulance crew looked at us incredulously as if we were acting a scene from *MASH*.

Jo did not move from the front door until the ambulance was on its way out of the drive.

In the hospital, I informed them that I had pneumonia and I wanted an immediate cure.

"How do you know that you have pneumonia? You probably have a bad attack of influenza."

"No, I have pneumonia."

Dr. Walsh had been sent for (he was our Palm Springs' doctor). He said, "You haven't got pneumonia but we'll have your lungs x-rayed."

All I could see was Jo's gaunt face and the tears in his eyes.

"Damn," I said, as they pushed the gurney into the x-ray room.

When they saw the results, they just looked at me and said, "How did you know?"

"How did I know what?"

"You have pneumonia?"

"Of course. Now, what is the quickest way to get rid of it? I took three Keflex as soon as I took my temperature. I want to get home as soon as possible."

"We'll have to enter you into the hospital."

"And do?"

"Well," said Dr. Walsh, now smiling, "We'll probably keep you on large doses of the Keflex you started yourself on."

"In that case, give me some and I'll handle it at home."

Vilma appeared. Jo had sent her down to see how I was. Poor, poor man, as if he didn't have enough problems. I wasn't going to add to them.

"Please, Dr. Walsh, I'll go anyway." He understood.

I was given the right amount of medication. I then got in the car with Vilma and returned to where I rightfully belonged.

I called Dr. Forde. He told me to stay in our room, and if my temperature went up, to telephone him as he might increase the medication. He also said drink honey and lemon and visit Jo once a day. I made a record recovery.

* * *

The awful food he had taken through his nose and the gentle walks around the house made Jo stronger. He had had that tracheotomy in his throat for a long time. We cleaned it twice a day, but, of course, he had to be checked every two months by Dr. Calcaterra. We also had a male nurse for a week from 9:00 A.M. to 5:00 P.M.

He came to me and said, "Since I've been here I've read three books. You and Vilma seem to be looking after him very well and he feels less sick with you. I don't know what the agency is charging you for me. It's bound to be too much. Of course, I'll stay if you want me to, I love it here, but it doesn't seem fair."

What a very nice man!

I thanked him profusely for I knew he meant it.

* * *

We had to go back and see Dr. Calcaterra. I booked a room at the Beverly Crest.

Dr. Calcaterra gave Jo about five minutes and said he saw more cancer.

When we returned to the hotel, Jo was particularly down and lost, so we telephoned Dr. Forde. I told him of Jo's sadness and our unsatisfactory visit.

He said, "I think it's time to see other doctors, get other opinions. A doctor-patient relationship is very important. Aside from Jo's failing voice, his speech is very slow since his stroke. I think he feels he's not getting enough time to ask some questions that are to him very important. I'll call Dr. Calcaterra and tell him what we are going to do."

Again we embarked on what we were sure would be a frustrating and depressing search. We saw several doctors, all very able and nice men, some suggested by Dr. Calcaterra.

On the way back from one of our appointments, Jo said, "Douglas, when you first told us the names of fine surgeons in California, didn't you mention a Dr. Rice?"

"Yes, Dr. Rice is the chief surgeon at USC and operates at Kenneth Norris Cancer Hospital. It's an excellent hospital at USC. It's just behind the County Hospital. If you wish to see him, I'll come with you, as Patricia will never find it."

We arranged a meeting for the following afternoon with Dr. Dale Rice.

* * *

Dr. Rice looked about fourteen years old. How could I put my husband in the hands of this child?

We had a long consultation. Jo asked a lot of questions, sometimes repeating them. The answers were explicit and clear. He was tolerant with Jo's hesitant speech and did not hurry him at all.

After examining him, he agreed with Dr. Calcaterra's diagnosis. He explained it fully. The larynx might have to be removed, but he was sure Dr. Calcaterra had done everything to save it and would continue to if it was possible, which I think he doubted. After listening to all he had to say, it was quite clear why he had reached the pinnacle of his profession. This was no child! He patted Jo on the shoulder and wished him luck.

As we left, Jo said to Douglas, "That is the first time I have felt any compassion."

It was obvious to me that Jo felt comfortable with the young-looking, understanding doctor. But as he drove us back, Douglas said, "I don't want you to make up your mind immediately, Jo. Sleep on it and tell me tomorrow afternoon who you have decided on."

There was no doubt in Jo's mind, nor for that matter, in mine.

The following afternoon, he made his decision known to Douglas Forde. Now it was up to Douglas to convince Dr. Rice to take Jo as a patient, do a biopsy on him and then?

* * *

Norris Hospital cared for patients with cancer. There are no questions they do not strive to answer. It was opened in 1983 at the University of Southern California and is also a research institute. There are only sixty patient rooms. The rest of the building is used for research.

It is really quite difficult to find (I got lost several times), but when you do find it, it is a haven for the sick and a comfort to their relatives.

On the day of the biopsy, I walked around the lounge, nervously pacing. I was not allowed to pace long. An attractive and efficient young lady called Becky invited me into her office.

"Do you want to talk?"

"No, thank you. I don't think so."

"Would you like some tea?"

I hesitated.

A charming dark-haired girl came in with a tray bearing a teapot with of all things, a cozy with a Union Jack as its pattern. Her name was Olga.

It was all helpful. I thanked them and went out to the lobby to pace again. Dr. Rice appeared and we sat down together. He told me he had seen the first culture and that it did not look good, but he would not have the definite one until later that night.

He told me I could go and see Jo. That night he called and said, "I'm afraid I've nothing but bad news for you. The cultures turned out positive."

"We expected that, didn't we?"

"Yes," he said. "I'm so sorry."

We set the date for the next operation.

"The main thing is to remove all the cancer. I'll try and save some of his larynx, but he must give me permission to remove it all if the cancer has spread."

"I'm sure he will," I replied.

We went to the hospital at 5:00 A.M. as the operation was to be at 6:30.

They let me stay with Jo until he was wheeled into surgery. The anesthetist came by, then Dr. Rice walked up to the gurney.

"I'm going to try and make you a well man again. If I have to remove the larynx, I will insert the little prosthesis in your throat. Remember you saw the lady talking on the video who was wearing it?"

Dr. Rice had gone to the trouble of bringing a television into Jo's room and played a video of a lady who'd had her larynx removed. Then she had a marvelous invention called a "Blom-Singer." It was a little prosthesis that was inserted into the esophagus, and, when one learned to use it, your own voice, only a little softer, came through the device. Two gentlemen, a Mr. Blom and a Mr. Singer, had invented it.

Jo nodded.

"I'll do my very best. Now, are there any last questions you'd like to ask me?"

"I don't like the way you worded that," replied my husband.

They all laughed — the young surgeon, the anesthetist and Jo, as they wheeled him away from me to his fate. Rice had faith, he had humor, but, most of all, he cared and Jo knew it.

* * *

It was a six-hour operation. My very dear friends, Bill Frye and James Wharton, arrived around noon to take me back to the hotel. They were surprised that he was still in surgery.

Out of nowhere appeared Dr. Rice. He looked for me and I ran to him.

"It was impossible to save the larynx, he had cancer on each side and in front and back. I removed it all. Of course, we'll know that later."

"My poor Jo," I said with painfully dry eyes.

"He's a marvelous man," said the doctor. He then looked at me very kindly and said, "He won't be in intensive care until after midnight. You mustn't wait. Have you anyone to be with?"

I pointed to Bill and Jim.

"Oh, good," he said.

"You've been through an awful lot." He put his arm around me and guided me towards my friends.

What had Jo said about compassion?

* * *

Back at the hotel, I couldn't eat. I went to my room to rest. Sleep was elusive.

It seemed he was days in Intensive Care, but there was always a nurse being kind and soothing. Also, we discovered another talented young doctor.

Dr. Eric Pinczower was so patient and attentive. I didn't notice that he looked even younger than Dr. Rice!

He informed me that they hoped to move Jo into his own room in the hospital the following day.

* * *

That evening, among the many messages that I received was one that I had to read out loud so I could believe it. It said: "Your sister will be arriving from England at 3:30 tomorrow!

I rang Bill Frye and shouted down the phone, "Piti's coming tomorrow!"

"What time and what airline? I'll go and meet her as you'll be at the hospital."

I couldn't wait for the morning to go and tell Jo, or for the afternoon when Bill would bring her to me.

Early in the evening, Gloria telephoned. She said Piti was coming alone for a week. Ken couldn't get away from his business. Gloria offered to keep her company, but between them they decided that they'd come separately as I would need Gloria's company later on.

I must mention here that if you poor readers are disappointed that these pages are not punctuated with famous names, you see, my brave husband and my family are the most important people I know.

The week with Piti went fast. We visited the hospital every day, and, Jo, trying to hide his emotion, kept squeezing her hands to convey his thanks. We'd sit in two little chairs facing him and he would gaze happily at the sisters. Then gesturing, he'd send us out. He didn't want me driving on two freeways in the dark.

* * *

Home! Oh, what letters and messages awaited us. Robert Goulet had called several times. I finally caught up with him and his Vera while he was touring in *Camelot*.

Anne Douglas wrote such a caring letter.

Anna Lee wrote him a lovely note. She is not too well, but working hard on *General Hospital*, and still finds time to write an old friend.

Katharine Hepburn wrote a long, marvelous letter. Their affection and respect for each other had started many years ago when they played on Broadway together in *The Philadelphia Story*. This is how she concluded her letter:

". . . Although we do not see each other often enough, I have a very warm place in my heart called Jo Cotten."

And he has one in his called Kate Hepburn.

For her to make that effort was so typical. Her manners, her talent and her smile have not lessened with the years. She will forever be unique.

They met many years ago while playing in Philadelphia Story, *but she still says she has a warm place in her heart called "Jo Cotten." And he had one in his called "Katharine Hepburn."/*

- 20 -

Amazing Grace

We have no doubt that he will be given a new voice.

We are blessedly lucky.

So many people are not as lucky as Jo. Think not that we are unaware of this. We are deeply aware, deeply concerned for them. We hold them in our thoughts and in our prayers.

Joseph Cotten is my husband. I know him better than I know anyone else, therefore, these words come from my selfish possessive heart.

I see his old movies and listen to that distinctive voice seldom. Only then I cry.

* * *

We stayed in the hotel as we had to now go three times a week to Dr. Daniel Kempler. He is a Ph.D., a rare teacher, patient, humorous and tenacious. The lessons are given in Dr. Rice's office at USC.

Jo found the lessons very difficult and painful. We spent weeks while he worked. He was tired and depressed.

For the first time I was beginning to think that Jo would never be able to learn to speak.

The little prosthesis that they had inserted after his voice box had been removed seemed not to be successful.

Every week he worked with Dr. Kempler, and although he tried most hard to give him confidence and teach him ever more patience, I could see that he was beginning to lose hope.

* * *

Dr. Rice telephoned. "Why hasn't he been to see me?"

I said, "He's upset and terribly disappointed. He absolutely cannot learn the lessons and he finds them most painful. I think we expected too much."

"Have you given up hope?" said Dr. Rice.

"Well, I worry about his discomfort with that prosthesis. I was going to order some more but I'm apprehensive. Jo is in such pain and he is, as you know, unbelievably brave. I wish I knew what to do."

"I want to see him at two o'clock tomorrow," he said.

I told Jo, and the following day we were back in the good doctor's office. He examined Jo thoroughly for at least an hour, after which he said that he thought he might be able to help him, but it would take another surgery.

Jo agreed, and within two days he was back in the operating room for a very long time. He would have to remain in the hospital for about five days because of the pain.

On the second day, I crept into his room. There stood my husband in jockey shorts, a vest and wearing his ascot.

"Good morning, darling. I'm ready to go home," he said.

I leaned against the door for support. Dr. Pinczower was there.

"I think you should put your pants on before leaving," said the doctor.

I telephoned Douglas Forde and handed the phone to Jo.

"Good morning, Douglas," said the actor, my husband.

I could hear Douglas' reaction from across the room.

* * *

I asked Dr. Rice to give me lessons on changing the prosthesis.

I was very quick at learning this delicate procedure. One strong reason is that Jo had complete faith in my ability and judgment while gently dealing with his problems. He simply couldn't conceive that I would let him down or pain him in any way, and he never knew how nervous I was.

Douglas told me that when a nurse was sticking a needle into his vein and taking some blood Jo said, "'Does my wife know you're doing this?" Poor nurse, who was very accomplished, looked bewildered!

Having gone through the lessons, I ordered two dozen to be sent home. If they need cleaning then it is done every day — but they last three weeks before changing. Of course, I could always telephone for more and very often did.

I found that Dr. Blom had an office in Santa Barbara, and that is where I telephoned for more Blom-Singers.

Feeling bold and indeed grateful, I telephoned Dr. Blom in Indianapolis, at his International Center for Post-Laryngectomy Voice Restoration, where he operated. He came to the phone. I told him who I was and congratulated him on his marvelous invention. I ended up by saying, "I think your office in Santa Barbara could use your attention."

He laughed and said, "It's not needed. It's doing very well, indeed."

"Still, sometimes I feel you should come out and see that it really is alright."

He laughed again and said he was glad we liked his work and he had new devices that were easier to use but that you had to have strong lungs."

"My husband's lungs are not too strong," I said, honestly.

"Call me if you need anything," he said.

"I just did," said the anxious wife before she hung up.

A week later, I had a telephone call from Dr. Blom from Santa Barbara! We went up and saw him. He looked like a movie star, not an inventor. He cheered my darling Jo.

Dr. Blom tried one of his newer models. It would have been very easy to use, but Jo's lungs were not strong enough.

* * *

We saw Dr. Rice again and did so once a week for a while.

Jo made an eloquent speech, thanking him for his persistence and his brilliant work, the result of which was manifest by the length of the speech.

Having said his say, we walked to the car. When we got in the car, I said:

"Hotel or Palm Springs, sir?"

"Palm Springs. *Home.*" He said clearly.

"Do you think it would be wise to rest your voice for most of the journey?"

"Why?"

"Because you are very excited and you'll want all our friends to hear you when we get there. Even the strongest, most natural voice tires. You have suffered so much torture to discover this lovely voice; don't over use it," I said.

"Patricia, stop the car."

I pulled over and he put his arm round me and kissed me gently. Then, he put his fingers to his lips, telling me he was going to be silent the rest of the way.

As soon as we arrived, he telephoned all our friends and asked them for drinks the following day!

It was a huge success!

We accepted several invitations to lunch and one or two to dinner.

That wonderful little prosthesis gave him such joy and confidence. Without realizing it, we forgot about the pain and fear and had gone back to our careless adventurous time and all our todays became yesterdays.

* * *

Jo enjoyed the Palm Springs social life, seeing all the kind people we knew for several weeks. He began to look tired. Actually, not so much tired as depressed.

This was not the time to tell him he ought to see Dr. Rice. He had said two months — so we still had time.

For days and nights I watched him carefully. He never complained, he smiled at me often, but the smile was not in his eyes.

One day he said quietly, "Poor little Patricia."

We were sitting on the bench in the galleria.

"Why, 'poor little Patricia?'" I said, apprehensively. "I'm completely happy and I want you to be."

"I don't expect I'll get any better than I am now. I seem to have gone down hill this past week."

"You're letting yourself get depressed again. We've been home quite a while. How can I help you?"

I saw the tears in his eyes as he touched my face and then the bell rang.

"Saved by the bell," said my husband as I went to answer the phone. It was Douglas checking.

I told him I thought Jo was getting depressed after being so happy.

"Why don't you go away for a couple of weeks? Go somewhere else and have some company; let someone new make an effort and cheer him up."

"Who can I get, and where can we go?" I cried, thrown by his sudden statement.

"You'll know," he replied.

Why oh why did he give me credit for knowing? At that moment I didn't know anything, and I certainly couldn't think of anywhere to go but home. I just couldn't think of anywhere to go or anyone to join us. Also, Jo, in his present mood, might be fearful.

I went outside and looked at his garden that the gardeners had not been treating very kindly. Jo was the best gardener of the lot, be it in the desert, in the country, near the sea or on a terrace. His artistic hands caressed the soil and planted trees, flowers and bushes.

Of course, he could no longer do it. There was so little that he could do. Most people in that condition would be frustrated and quite often bad tempered.

I looked at our Mesquite tree and said, "Help me — please help me." Actually, I was talking to myself . . .

* * *

Our very good friend, Rosalie Hearst, who had a home in Palm Springs, telephoned to invite us with a few mutual friends to spend a week at Wyntoon, a fairyland consisting of over 80,000 acres of timberland and about ten houses (called cottages).

William Randolph Hearst's mother had discovered it and built a house (that turned into a castle) there. Later, W.R. himself (as he is referred to by the family) built all the rest, a huge swimming pool, a projection room, an office for himself and the cottages for the family.

"Rosalie, it sounds absolutely lovely, but do you think Jo will be alright there?"

"Of course he will, he doesn't have to walk at all if he can't or doesn't want to. We all have cars. He must eat with us, though, meals are the only rules. The weather is clear and beautiful."

"We'd just love it," I tried to say but she interrupted me.

"I haven't finished. After a week, we'll all go to San Simeon for another week, same rules, meals together."

I didn't even ask Jo, after all, our doctor had confidence and told me that "I'd know." It was a heaven-sent invitation.

Rosalie Hearst is the widow of George Hearst, who was one of the great man's sons. She is delicately lovely in a most refined way. Jo loves her and feels so happy in her company. What could go wrong? Nothing. Nothing went wrong at all.

* * *

We drove up to Wyntoon. My friend, Marion Lederer and I shared the driving. She is the wife of screen star Francis Lederer. Jo sat in the back with loads of maps and was the navigator. We stopped for the night in Sacramento and had sandwiches in the room of our very dark hotel. Daylight came and we were on our way, again.

The following evening we arrived in Fairyland. Jo and I were given the bridal suite in Cinderella Cottage!

Rosalie's house was River House. Sitting on the terrace before dinner with the McCloud River flowing peacefully below was like being in another world.

Each day Jo seemed stronger. The Blom-Singer was a great success.

I asked Rosalie if she noticed any improvement. She said she had most certainly, but she didn't want to say anything in case it went wrong.

The week was gone in a flash.

* * *

Jo and I left a day early for San Simeon and spent the night at the Wonderland Motel.

In San Simeon we all stayed at the Ranch which was William Randolph Hearst's mother's house. It is called Pheobe's House (which was her name).

The Castle was above us, gleaming at night, in all its magnificence. "Xanadu," whispered Jo.

It is the most thrilling place to visit. Rosalie arranged for us all to go on a private tour. Jo had stayed there years ago when Bill Hearst lived there and before it was given to the State. This did not prevent him from touring it all once again. Only this time in a wheelchair.

After we had returned, he received several letters from people who had seen him there.

They, of course, were interested in seeing him *there* of all places, because of *Citizen Kane*.

Kane had been reported to be based on the life of William Randolph Hearst. Orson denied this, but many people did not believe him, including, most important of all, the Hearst Press. Orson and all the actors paid the price. Hearst's power was so strong. Jo starred in several pictures after the making of *Kane*, and the Hearst papers reviewed the pictures without mentioning his name.

Apparently after quite a while all was forgotten—at least by Hearst's sons. Orson made several other masterpieces. Hollywood didn't treat him fairly. He was brilliant. His daughter Beatrice is beautiful and clever. She always called Jo her "kissing cousin."

* * *

Our return from San Simeon was easy. We broke the trip at a place called "The Honeymoon Motel." If the name was meant to reflect on its owners someone had played a cruel joke, for a more argumentative couple I have yet to meet. They recognized Jo and spent quite a while discussing how much to charge him. Every time "she" opened her mouth, "he" said —

"Shut up, you silly bitch. Leave this to me."

"Let's give them the bridal suite upstairs. That will be $120.00 paid in advance."

"I think I could handle the bridegroom part, but I'm not sure about the stairs," said Jo, amicably.

"I think we should leave," said I. "There are plenty of honest people further down the road, and we're not in a hurry."

"You stupid bastard. You've gone and screwed it," she said.

"Oh, if it's just a room you want, I have a very nice one downstairs for $60.00. Two king-sized beds, sir."

"We'll take it," said Jo, coldly.

As soon as we got to our bargain digs, I said, "Why didn't we walk out, Jo? That's not like you."

"Because I know this road very well and there isn't another motel for many miles. There was one closer but it's just closed, maybe Romeo and Juliet don't know. Also, Patricia, I looked at your little face. You're very pale and very tired. If only I hadn't had that awful stroke I could drive."

Of course he was right. He was always right. I was tired. We left early the next morning and went straight home.

* * *

When we got home, Jo played the butler — we drank a toast to each other.

"Did you enjoy your holiday?" I said.

"Yes. That's what it was, a holiday — and I enjoyed every minute of it, especially not having any fearful nightmares. Just you and the McCloud River beside me."

He had a little color back in his cheeks and his eyes were shining.

Something new that I have learned in the past few years is that illness, not necessarily serious illness, leaves one depressed. In former years, after anything like what Jo had gone through, people were sent to convalescent homes. They were not yet ready to cope with "getting better" without professional help. Even if the body is cured, the mind suffers a reaction. It is asking to get away from it all, to forget the recent trauma and to bring laughter back into your life.

Our vacation sounds special, but the real specialty about it was the simplicity.

Good home cooking, walks for people who wanted exercise, drives to the village store for those who were adventurous. Plenty of rest and fresh air. In other words, we were living in the "slow lane." *But*, we were living.

- 21 -

The Light That Didn't Fail

I shouldn't have been surprised to come home one day and find him in the galleria with steel and copper and wood, and a work bench and paint, but I was.

"I thought you were in bed," I said sternly, as sternly as if I were speaking to a little boy playing with his toys.

"I can't very well do this sculpturing in bed," as he worked away. "You see, Patricia, I'm no good on my legs, my voice is failing fast. I can't work on my speech. I can only really use my hands and my imagination. So you see before you, darling, Joseph Cotten, sculptor.

For several months, Michelangelo worked in the galleria.

Oh, I know that I'm prejudiced, *but* he modeled an accumulation of interesting, shapely, yet quite modern sculptures.

They all have names, he has signed them, and he intends to have a showing. If he is strong enough, he surely will.

But always he needed a rest between modeling his talent. Was it over-excitement or overwork? He became less energetic. He became weak.

* * *

Back to the phone. I sent a telephonic cardiogram. With a gadget the cardiologist had given me, I managed to test his hearbeat and then his pacemaker. It didn't seem right. His pacemaker was weakening.

Naturally, we went to St. John's to have it changed. Virginia put a cot in his room for me.

He found this operation a monumental strain.

As I held his hands, he whispered to me, "Darling, however ill I get, will you make me a promise?"

"Of course."

"I do not want ever to be in a hospital again. I've had too much hospitalization. Promise me?"

"I promise."

* * *

He got a little stronger, but Palm Springs seemed to me to be too far from his own physician. He and I both sensed he would need Douglas.

We sold the useless, beautiful house and garden and his blessed pool in Palm Springs and bought a large condo on Wilshire Boulevard.

We made it look beautiful. The more beautiful it became, the weaker he became. It wasn't his pacemaker. He was getting thinner and thinner.

Douglas told me that after the pacemaker had been changed, they had taken a bone scan because of the loss of weight. (He waited to tell me as I was too upset.) The cancer had spread to his prostate and up to his bones, and, I believe, to the spine.

I knew he must not know this and that I had to take him home as promised. Home, of course, was to our now beautiful apartment.

* * *

It became necessary to change the Blom-Singer every two days. He hadn't the strength in his lungs to assist his esophagus. He lay on the bed exhausted.

"I hate to say this, but would you feel better in the hospital?"

"No."

"Would you accept some nurses here. I'd be with you all the time and you would have all your things around you to help you get better?"

A tiny nod of approval.

* * *

We had excellent nurses twenty-four hours a day. He did not complain. He had to have a hospital bed (which he hated), but again he did not complain. He was surrounded by the colors of the pictures in his room. The nurses reassured him that he

Robert Wagner and his wife, Jill St. John.

was at home. His mind throughout all his suffering remained clear, and his brain was not affected, ever.

Dr. Forde came every day, and his visits were like Christmas. He always answered Jo's questioning speech or gaze (the latter was probably more understandable), and he thought of a reason why he was feeling so ill and why he had to take it gently to get better.

Douglas is a lousy liar. I think Jo knew it. I also know Jo knew that Douglas would do everything humanly possible to save him — even if it was too late. Jo wanted to hear his voice and hold his healing hand that said he cared and in its helpless way, helped him.

* * *

Oh — how pleased he was when he saw friends, just for a short while.

I told some close friends how ill he was and if they could come up for about ten minutes it would be just fine.

I was disappointed that some of them said, "Oh, I don't want to see him. I want to remember him as he was."

Disappointment from me, but no argument — some people cannot take it.

Bill Frye and James Wharton bought a beautiful tree and carried it into his bedroom. He loved it.

Ruthie and Carl Esmond popped in often.

Jennifer, of course, came. She saw him in the mirror, trying to put a loose Ascot round his throat to hide the entrance to the Blom-Singer. She delayed her own entrance, calmly walked in and said just the right things.

Jennifer is not scared of anything. Surprise? Not to us — she made up for a lot of people who were too upset to come or thought he'd be upset by seeing them.

Didn't they realize that the more desperately ill he became, the more beautiful he looked? Such smooth skin, still that hair shining, and from his exquisitely thin face gazed two El Greco eyes, smiling when he saw a friend, huge and frightened when alone.

Wonderful, loyal, decent and brave Robert Wagner came to see him on Christmas Day. He stayed as long as he was allowed which was longer than anyone else would have been permitted.

I gave Jo a new prosthesis and he was proudly able to carry on a conversation with the fine actor and reminisce about working together.

"We did have fun, didn't we?" said Bob.

"We didn't have long enough," said my sweet husband.

Wagner said he'd come and see him again, and Jo asked him to bring Jill (St. John), his wife with whom Jo had worked.

What we didn't know was that Jill was downstairs in the lobby all the time that her husband was upstairs. She wasn't sure whether Jo was up to seeing two people. What a fine, sensitive and beautiful person she is!

Robert J. Wagner was his last guest. I can never thank him enough, or Jill. As he was leaving, he said, "He's an example to everyone." He quickly walked out of the door. He was crying.

* * *

Even though there was always a nurse beside him, I never undressed at night. I'd take a bath around 3:00 A.M. when Jo's medication seemed to allow him to sleep. Then I'd put makeup and clothes on, and change if and when I could. A robe and a sad pale face might make him even weaker. You see, he never ceased worrying about me, so I covered my fear.

Have I mentioned that he was unique? Once in a while, while he was sleeping, I'd go and lie on the bed in his dressing room. Try to read. Try not to think.

"Mrs. Cotten, maybe you'd better come back, I don't like his breathing," said the night nurse, softly, at 6:00 A.M.

I was at his side in an instant. His eyes were closed but I think he knew I was there.

I kissed him on the lips. He gave a faint sigh which I breathed. It was his soul. He gave it to me.

I ran and opened the window. To try to stop him? To join him?

A gentle breeze sent a warm cloak around my shoulders — I looked up.

A faint light twinkled in the sky. I gazed at it and whispered, "Life after life. Eternally."

* * *

Joseph Cotten left this world February 6, 1994. age 88

* * *

I woke this morning to a glorious morn,

And ached because my life was so forlorn

Is there no cure for my malaise,

That saddens all my nights and days?

Oh God, please tell me what to do

And then — I thought about you . . .

P. M. C.

Appendix

Patricia Medina's credits include:

Films:	*Starred with:*
Don't Take It to Heart	Richard Greene
Hotel Reserve	Herbert Lom
The Day Will Dawn	Deborah Kerr & Hugh Williams
Moss Rose	Peggy Cummins
Foxes of Harrow	Sir Rex Harrison & Maureen O'Hara
Snow White and the Three Stooges	
The Lady in the Iron Mask	Louis Hayward
Stranger at My Door	Macdonald Carey
Duel on the Mississippi	Dennis O'Keefe
Mrs. Arkadin	Orson Welles
Dick Curtin	Louis Hayward
Rx Murder (later *Columbo* series)	Joseph Cotten
Secret Heart	Walter Pidgeon, Claudette Colbert, & June Allyson
Three Musketeers	Gene Kelly & June Allyson
Desperate Search	Howard Keel & Jane Greer
Miami Expose	Lee J. Cobb
Valentino	Anthony Dexter & Eleanor Parker
Jackpot	James Stewart
Botany Bay	Alan Ladd & James Mason
Sangaree	Fernando Lamas & Arlene Dahl
Plunder of the Sun	Glenn Ford
The Black Knight	Alan Ladd
Killing of Sister George	Beryl Reid & Susannah York
Murder in the Rue Morgue	Karl Malden & Steve Forrest
Francis	Donald O'Connor
Latitude Zero	Joseph Cotten & Cesar Romero
Timber Tramp	Joseph Cotten & Cesar Romero

Television:	*Starred with:*
Rawhide	Clint Eastwood
The Rogues	Charles Boyer
The Thriller	
Man From U.N.C.L.E.	

Broadway: ***Starred with:***
Calculated Risk   Joseph Cotten
Seven Ways of Love

National Theatre:
Toured w/Joseph Cotten in *Marriage Go Round* & *Reluctant Debutante*

Film Career Achievement Award from Society for Cinephiles, 1997

Index

About the Author

London-born movie star Patricia Medina, one of the world's great beauties, decided to write her autobiography as a catharsis following the death of her husband the noted actor Joseph Cotten (star of such immortal films as *Citizen Kane* and *The Third Man*). Hers was one of the great love matches in Hollywood history and she felt that by reliving her past she could overcome of the grief which followed her tragic loss.

Thus three years later, *Laid Back In Hollywood* has arrived at the bookstores and Patricia is ready to resume a life knowing that her experiences with the Who's Who of Hollywood and her 30 year marriage to Jo Cotten can be shared by friends and fans alike.

Having appeared in more than 20 films before arriving in Hollywood, Patricia, a product of a British mother and Spanish father, grew up in England and France becoming a language specialist in French, Italian, Spanish and of course English.

As a teenager, she met the American producer Joe Rock at Elstree Studios, near London, who gave her a screen test and offered a film contract which her parents vetoed. Determined on a film career, Patricia received her parents permission to appear in a J. Arthur Rank religious film.

But it was not long before she was in commercial plays, films and radio without parental fuss. At the close of World War II she was an established film star touring France, Holland, Belgium and Germany appearing in plays for Allied troops.

Patricia's American screen debut was in MGM's *The Secret Heart* with Claudette Colbert, Walter Pidgeon and June Allyson followed by films at Columbia, Fox and Universal.

She became famed as a classic screen beauty without a single bad camera angle but she rebelled at not being allowed to play comedy. As she said, "I'm fed up portraying the femme fatale who must come to a dismal end. I've been drowned, strangled, shot and burned to death and even killed with poison tea. I want to play everything for laughs—even murder scenes."

There followed a succession of films including *Foxes of Harrow, Phantom of the Rue Morgue, Black Knight, Stranger At My Door,* and *The Killing of Sister George.*

Her second marriage—the first to Richard Greene of *Robin Hood* fame—to Joseph Cotten was the crowning moment of her life. For 30 years they romanced, travelled abroad, acted together and their dramatic story became the culmination of her book *Laid Back In Hollywood.* This, together with reminiscences of most of the great stars of Hollywood including Gable, Olivier, Cary Grant, Jennifer Jones, Jimmy Stewart, Orson Welles, Louis B. Mayer, Gregory Peck, Fred Astaire, Cole Porter and Rex Harrison, to mention a few, gives one a fascinating insight of the great days of Tinseltown. Miss Medina resides in Beverly Hills,California.